THE MYSTERY OF THE HOLY SPIRIT

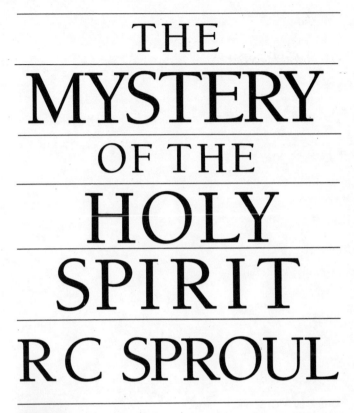

THE
MYSTERY
OF THE
HOLY
SPIRIT
R C SPROUL

Tyndale House Publishers, Inc. Wheaton, Illinois

For Judy

R.C. Sproul

For Michael Jeffrey Dick

Quotations from John Calvin's *Institutes* are the Henry
Beveridge translation (Grand Rapids: Eerdmans, 1964).

Scripture quotations are taken from The New King
James Version. Copyright © 1979, 1980, 1982,
Thomas Nelson Inc., Publishers.

Library of Congress Catalog Card Number 89-51634
ISBN 0-8423-4617-1 (HC)
ISBN 0-8423-4378-4 (SC)

Printed in the United States of America

00 99 98 97 96 95 94
 7   6   5   4   3   2   1

CONTENTS

PREFACE

"The Holy Spirit leaves no footprints in the sand." These words are from Abraham Kuyper's classic work on the Holy Spirit. Jesus did leave footprints in the sand. He was God incarnate, God with a human nature. When His disciples walked with Him, they could hear His voice, touch His hands, and watch the sand spilling over His feet as He trod the shores of the Sea of Galilee.

But the Holy Spirit is like the wind. Jesus said, "The wind blows where it wishes, and you hear the sound of it, but cannot tell where it comes from and where it goes" (John 3:8). We cannot capture the wind in a bottle. It is elusive and mysterious but nonetheless real. We see the effects of the wind—trees bending and swaying in the breeze, flags rustling. We see the devastation of the fierce hurricane. We see the ocean become violent in a gale. We are refreshed by gentle zephyrs on a summer day. We know the wind is there.

So it is with the Holy Spirit. He is intangible and invisible. But His work is more powerful than the most ferocious wind. The Spirit brings order out of chaos and beauty out of ugliness. He can transform a sin-blistered man into a paragon of virtue. The Spirit changes people. The Author of life is also the Transformer of life.

Because the Spirit is mysterious, we are vulnerable to

superstitions and distortions of His person and work. Here we must listen carefully to Scripture as it reveals to us the character of God the Holy Spirit.

This book is about Him, the Third Person of the Holy Trinity. The book is written for the serious layperson and seeks to avoid undue theological technicalities. Some sections will require deep thought. Some probe the abstract because it is unavoidable if we are to grow in our understanding of the Spirit.

The book is written for those who desire a deeper spiritual life, a result that cannot happen apart from the Spirit, the One who sanctifies.

Orlando, Easter 1989

CHAPTER ONE

WHO IS THE HOLY SPIRIT?

He who does not know
God the Holy Spirit
cannot know God at all.
THOMAS ARNOLD

THE POETS tell us that in the spring a young man's fancy turns to love. In the spring of 1958 my fancy was locked in mortal conflict. It was a conflict between my mortal manhood and God's immortal law, a battle that no man can ever fully or finally win.

I was experiencing my own private "High Noon." If I remember the words from the theme song of Gary Cooper's cinematic classic, they went something like this:

Oh, to be torn between love and duty:
supposin' I lose my fair-haired beauty.
Look at that big hand move along . . .
nearin' high noon . . .

My beauty was not fair-haired, but all the rest fit my circumstances. I was torn between love and duty, and the clock was racing toward noon.

In 1952 I fell in love. In the spring of 1957 I gave my girlfriend a diamond ring. We were engaged to be married. The wedding was scheduled for June 1960.

All our dreams and plans for marriage were jolted by an unexpected shock wave that hit us in the fall of 1957. I was suddenly, violently (in a spiritual sense) converted to Christ. I rushed to give my fiancée my joyous news. I could hardly wait to share my newfound faith with her in the full expectation that she would immediately embrace the Lord with me.

I poured out the story of my conversion to her. I was

effervescent with spiritual enthusiasm. I had found the pearl of great price and was extolling the wonders of its opulence to her.

She was unimpressed. It was like trying to describe a kaleidoscope to a blind man. She listened politely but maintained a remote aloofness to the subject. She took refuge in the hope that I was experiencing a "phase," a flirtation with some kind of temporary religious madness.

"What do you mean that you've become a Christian?" she asked. "You have always been a Christian. You were baptized, confirmed, and all the rest."

She had been confirmed in the same church in which I had. We sang in the choir together. We went to youth fellowship together. We learned to dance at the church socials together. Now I was talking about being "born again." This was a phrase she had never heard. This was pre-Jimmy Carter, pre-Chuck Colson, before the phrase *born again* invaded the lexicon of popular culture. In 1958 the phrase conveyed to my fiancée a signal of fanaticism that represented a clear and dangerous threat to our relationship.

As the months passed, what I hoped would enhance my relationship with my fiancée instead prompted a severe strain. I soon discovered that not many people shared my enthusiasm about being born again. My mother felt I was rejecting her and her values. My sister was hostile. My friends were incredulous. My minister, of all people, called me "a damn fool."

I was beginning to learn the tensions created by differences of belief and understanding of Christianity. I was also beginning to learn the commandments, not only of Moses but of Christ. The worst rule, the rule that riled my soul, was the one about being "unequally yoked." I was instructed that a believer was not permitted to marry an unbeliever.

But I was in love with an unbeliever. I was engaged to an unbeliever. I was being torn between love and duty.

I tried to bargain with God. I made a vow to Him. I vowed that if my girlfriend did not become a Christian by the end of a weekend visit she was making to my college, I would break up with her.

I didn't tell her about my vow. I didn't tell anybody about it. It was a private pact between me and the Almighty.

On the morning of the day she was scheduled to arrive, I locked myself in my room and entered into a vigil of intercessory prayer. I made the pleas of the importunate widow in Jesus' parable seem mild by comparison. Had an angel been present with which to wrestle, I would have left the mat a paraplegic. I knew nothing of election or of eternal decrees. If God didn't have my fiancée's name in the Book of Life, *I* wanted it inscribed there that very day. The violent were taking the kingdom of God by force. Or at least I was trying to.

That night she attended a prayer meeting with me. She was reluctant. She was suspicious. She was frustrated by my insistence that she go with me to "this religious thing."

In the middle of the prayer meeting, she, like John

Wesley at Aldersgate, felt her heart "strangely warmed." Like Augustine in the garden and Martin Luther in the tower, she saw the gates of paradise swing open, and she walked through.

After the meeting, with an excitement that exceeded my own, she said these exact words: "Now I know who the Holy Spirit is."

This comment does not reflect the analysis of a trained theologian. It is the observation of a fresh convert to the Christian faith. I think, however, that it merits some exposition. It is a spontaneous response to a life-changing experience, and it carries the insight of a first-glance, virgin response to faith.

As simple as the statement sounds, it carries some profound insights. Let us examine it closely, then.

The first word is significant. "Now," she said. *Now* refers to the present time. The clear implication is that the *now* stands in sharp contrast to what went before. The *now* calls attention to something new that was not present in the *then*.

When my fiancée made this statement, she explained that in the past she had heard of the Holy Spirit. The Holy Spirit was mentioned in church. The trinitarian formula "In the name of the Father, the Son, and the Holy Ghost" was heard frequently at weddings, in the words of the sacraments of baptism and the Lord's Supper, in benedictions, and in the closing words of the pastoral prayer.

Yet in her church experience, the words *Holy Spirit* simply referred to a vague, abstract part of the liturgy.

The name, or title, of the Third Person of the Trinity had no concrete meaning to her.

The word *know* signaled a dawn of recognition. Suddenly, an awareness broke through, an awareness that was previously veiled by abstraction: "Now I *know*," she declared.

When Vesta (my fiancée) added "I know," she was confessing a new kind of knowledge. Again, this was not the first time she had ever heard of the Holy Spirit. She was familiar with the language. She had taken the catechism tests. She possessed some cognitive awareness of the Holy Spirit.

"Now I know" indicates a new kind of knowledge, a knowledge that passes beyond the cognitive to the personal and experiential kind of knowledge.

This statement calls to mind the apostolic teaching regarding spiritual awareness. Paul declares to the Corinthians:

"Eye has not seen, nor ear heard, nor have entered into the heart of man, the things which God has prepared for those who love Him." But God has revealed them to us through His Spirit. For the Spirit searches all things, yes, the deep things of God. For what man knows the things of a man except the spirit of a man which is in him? Even so no one knows the things of God except the Spirit of God. Now we have received, not the spirit of the world, but the Spirit who is from God, that we might know the things that have been freely given to us by God. These things we also speak, not in words which man's wisdom teaches but which the Holy Spirit teaches, comparing spiritual things with spiritual. But the natural man does not receive the things of

*the Spirit of God, for they are foolishness to him; nor can
he know them, because they are spiritually discerned.*
(1 Corinthians 2:9-14)

This passage is so crucial for our understanding of
the Holy Spirit that we will return to it later for a fuller
exposition. However, we note at present that Paul
speaks here of a kind of spiritual discernment that is not
"natural" to us. That is, in our fallen human state we
lack the ability to receive the things of God. Indeed,
Paul emphatically declares: "nor can he know them."

It is impossible for an unspiritual person to discern
spiritual things. We are not by nature spiritual persons.
A person cannot discern spiritual things until that person is first made alive to spiritual things by the Spirit of
God. It is the Spirit's work of regeneration, of spiritual
rebirth, that enables us to have spiritual discernment.

When Vesta said, "Now I know," she was con-
sciously—or unconsciously—bearing witness to her
new spiritual state, her conversion.

"Now I know who the Holy Spirit is."

It is significant that Vesta did not say, "Now I know
what the Holy Spirit is." She knew *who* He was. Her
initial awareness of God the Holy Spirit in her life was
an awareness of a personal presence.

The Bible reveals the Holy Spirit not as an "it" (an
abstract force, power, or thing) but as "He." The Holy
Spirit is a person. Personality includes intelligence, will,
and individuality. A person acts with intentionality. No
abstract force can ever "intend" to do anything. Good

or bad intentions are limited to the powers of personal beings.

THE BIBLE USES PERSONAL PRONOUNS FOR THE HOLY SPIRIT.

When we speak about persons we use words such as *I*, *you*, *he*, and *she*. There are times, of course, when such words are used for impersonal objects or things. We use gender terms for such things as boats or cars or the church. Normally this is done in clearly recognizable ways. Personification is also a useful tool for poetic expressions.

However, when the Scriptures use personal pronouns for the Holy Spirit, they do so in passages that are not poetic but narrative and didactic. In Acts 13:2, we read:

As they ministered to the Lord and fasted, the Holy Spirit said, "Now separate to Me Barnabas and Saul for the work to which I have called them."

We note here the use of the words *Me* and *I* ascribed to the Holy Spirit. We note also in passing that in this text the Holy Spirit speaks and gives intelligible, intentional instructions. We observe a similar occurrence in John 15:26:

But when the Helper comes, whom I shall send to you from the Father, the Spirit of truth, who proceeds from the Father, He will testify of Me.

Here Jesus refers to the Spirit as *whom* and as *He*. Some scholars may reply that in this text the Greek word for Helper is not the masculine gender and that, according to the rules of grammar, the pronoun must agree with the noun in gender. However, there is an intervening clause ("the Spirit of truth who . . . ") that uses the neuter gender for Spirit. It is followed immediately by the word *He*. If the writer meant for the Spirit to be thought of as an impersonal neuter force there would be no reason to use the masculine pronoun *He* in such close conjunction with a neuter noun.

If the matter is unclear in John 15, it is crystal clear in John 16:13:

When He, the Spirit of truth, has come, He will guide you into all truth; for He will not speak on His own authority, but whatever He hears He will speak; and He will tell you things to come.

Here there is no grammatical reason whatsoever to use the masculine pronoun *He* unless Jesus intends in this didactic passage to declare that the Holy Spirit is a person.

WE ARE CALLED INTO A PERSONAL RELATIONSHIP WITH THE HOLY SPIRIT.

The Bible calls us to "believe" in the Holy Spirit. We are baptized into His name as well as the name of the Father and the Son. The Spirit is an object of prayer. Believers are not to address "things" in prayer. To do so would be an act of idolatry. We are only to address God, who is personal.

The apostolic benediction in the New Testament includes reference to fellowship and communion with the Holy Spirit:

The grace of the Lord Jesus Christ, and the love of God, and the communion of the Holy Spirit be with you all.
(2 Corinthians 13:14)

The New Testament exhorts us not to sin against the Holy Spirit, not to resist the Holy Spirit, and not to grieve the Holy Spirit. He is set forth as a person whom we may either please or offend, who can love and be loved, and with whom we can have personal fellowship.

THE HOLY SPIRIT PERFORMS PERSONAL TASKS.
The Holy Spirit relates to us as a person. He does things to us and for us, things that we normally associate with personal activity. He teaches us. He comforts us. He guides us. He encourages us.

These activities can be achieved at times by impersonal objects. Mariners can be "guided" by stars. We can take comfort by contemplating a beautiful sunset. But the comfort derived from such contemplation is based on a conscious or unconscious assumption that behind the sunset is a Personal Artist of the sunset. We can be "taught" by observing natural objects, but only by way of analogy.

The way in which the Spirit comforts, guides, teaches, etc., is a personal way. As He performs these tasks, the Bible describes His activity as involving intelligence, will, feeling, and power. The Spirit searches, selects, reveals, and admonishes. Stars and sunsets do not behave this way.

In summary, we conclude that if the Holy Spirit can

be loved, adored, obeyed, offended, grieved, or sinned against, He must be a person.

But the question still remains: Is the Holy Spirit a distinct person? Does He have a personality that may be distinguished from that of God the Father and God the Son? Do all of the personal qualities the Bible attributes to Him really refer to the personality of the Father, with the Spirit being simply an aspect of the Father?

These questions immediately raise the problem of how we are to think about God. Do we believe in one God or three Gods? The mysterious and difficult idea of the Trinity intrudes into our thinking the moment we begin to think about the Holy Spirit as a distinct person. It is the classical faith of the church that the Holy Spirit is not only a person; He is a divine person; He is God.

CHAPTER TWO

THE
HOLY
SPIRIT
IS
GOD

Every time we say,
"I believe in the Holy Spirit,"
we mean that we believe
that there is a living God
able and willing to enter
human personality and change it.

J. B. PHILLIPS

W E have seen that the Bible reveals that the Holy Spirit is a person, not a thing. We call Him *He* rather than *It*. At the same time, the Bible reveals also that the Holy Spirit is a *divine* person. He is God. This chapter—and the rest of this book—will affirm this over and over. But before we can look at the Holy Spirit as God, we must first look at Jesus Christ as God.

For centuries there have been bitter quarrels concerning the deity of Jesus. In every generation there have been efforts to reduce Jesus to the level of one who is merely human. The confession of the church has been that Christ is the God-man, one person with two natures, human and divine. At the Council of Chalcedon in A.D. 451 the church declared that Jesus was truly man (*vere homo*) and truly God (*vere deus*).

Four centuries in church history have been marked by severe debates about the deity of Christ. These were the fourth century, the fifth century, the nineteenth century, and the twentieth century. I mention this because we happen to be living in one of the centuries in which the deity of Christ has been most hotly disputed. (Indeed, the book *The Myth of God Incarnate*, which seriously questioned Jesus' deity, was popular a few years ago. Sadly, it was not written by those outside the church but, rather, by respected teachers of theology.) Christ is seen variously as the greatest of men, a unique prophet, the supreme example of ethics, a model of existential "authenticity," a symbol of human revolutionary spirit, an angel power, and even an "adopted" son of God. All of these designations, however, usually include the idea that Jesus is a *creature*, a man (or angel) created by God. All of these views include the idea that Christ had a beginning in space and time. They deny His eternality and coessentiality with God.

Some modern religions exalt the person of Jesus so that He functions as a focal point of religious devotion despite the fact that He is seen as a creature. The Mormons and Jehovah's Witnesses both regard Jesus as a created being, yet they give considerable devotion to Him. If such devotion involves actual worship, then we must sadly conclude that these religions are, at the core, idolatrous. Idolatry means giving worship to someone or something other than the Eternal God. Idolatry involves the worship of creatures. Mormonism may insist that Jesus is the Creator of the world, yet His act of creation follows upon His own creation by God. The idea is something like this: God created Jesus, then Jesus created the world. Here Jesus is both Creator and creature.

If Jesus is not God, then it follows that orthodox Christianity is at root heretical. It does violence to the oneness of God and ascribes worship to the Son and to the Holy Spirit, who are not divine. If, on the other hand, the Son and the Holy Spirit are in fact divine, then we must conclude that Jehovah's Witnesses are

Jehovah's *false* witnesses and that Mormonism is a non-Christian heretical sect.

Though there are many, indeed far too many, Christian denominations, most of them recognize the others as being *true*, though imperfect, forms of Christian expressions. Baptists generally consider Presbyterians to be valid expressions of the universal Christian church. Presbyterians acknowledge that Lutherans are indeed Christians.

The assumption among various Christian bodies is that though they differ from other Christian bodies on some doctrinal points, these particular points are not absolutely essential to true Christianity. It is because the deity of Christ and of the Holy Spirit are regarded as essential affirmations to biblical Christianity that most orthodox Christians do not recognize either Mormonism or Jehovah's Witnesses as Christian churches. The same would be said of Unitarianism, which also denies the deity of the Son and the Holy Spirit.

As fierce as the debates have been regarding the deity of Christ, there has been comparatively little controversy with respect to the deity of the Holy Spirit. The Bible so clearly represents the Holy Spirit as possessing divine attributes and exercising divine authority that since the fourth century His deity has rarely been denied by those who agree that He is a person. That is, though there have been many disputes concerning the question of whether the Spirit is a person or an impersonal "force," once it is admitted that He is indeed a person, the fact that He is a *divine* person falls easily into place.

(This is not too surprising; after all, the Spirit, since He has never assumed human form as the Son did, could not possibly be "just a human being," which is what many heresies say about Jesus Christ. A Spirit must, obviously, be a spiritual being.)

In the Scripture we see a frequent allusion to the deity of the Holy Spirit. In the Old Testament, for example, what is said of God is also said of the Spirit of God. The expressions "God said" and "the Spirit said" are repeatedly interchanged. The activity of the Holy Spirit is said to be the activity of God.

The same phenomena occur in the New Testament. In Isaiah 6:9 God speaks and says, "Go and tell this people." The apostle Paul quotes this text in Acts 28:25 and introduces it by saying: "The Holy Spirit spoke rightly through Isaiah the prophet to our fathers." Here the Apostle ascribes the speaking of God to the Holy Spirit.

Likewise the Apostle declares that believers are the temple of God because the Holy Spirit dwells in us. (See Ephesians 2:22; 1 Corinthians 6:19; Romans 8:9-10.) If the Holy Spirit Himself is not God, how could we properly be called the temple of God simply because the Holy Spirit dwells in us? One could answer this question by arguing that the Holy Spirit is sent by God and therefore represents God. This would simply mean that where God is represented by one of His active agents it may be said that God is "there." To reach this conclusion, however, is to play loosely with the plain meaning of the text. Throughout Scripture the Holy Spirit is identified with God Himself, not merely portrayed as a delegated representative of God.

In Acts 5:3-4 we read:

Peter said, "Ananias, why has Satan filled your heart to lie to the Holy Spirit and keep back part of the price of the land for yourself? . . . You have not lied to men but to God."

Here we see an equation: A lie to the Holy Spirit is a lie to God Himself.

Christ and the apostles repeatedly describe the Holy Spirit as One who possesses divine attributes and perfections. Blasphemy against the Holy Spirit is deemed the unforgivable sin. Were the Holy Spirit not God, it is extremely unlikely that blasphemy against Him would be regarded as unpardonable.

The Holy Spirit is *omniscient*. He knows all. Here we see the Spirit possessing an attribute of God. Omniscience is a mark of the Deity, not of creatures. Creatures are limited by time and space. These limits impose a limitation on the extent of their knowledge. Paul declares:

The Spirit searches all things, yes, the deep things of God. For what man knows the things of a man except the spirit of the man which is in him? Even so no one knows the things of God except the Spirit of God. (1 Corinthians 2:10-11)

The Holy Spirit is *omnipresent*. The psalmist asks rhetorically:

Where can I go from Your Spirit? Or where can I flee from Your presence? If I ascend into heaven, You are there;

27

if I make my bed in hell, behold, You are there. (Psalm 139:7-8)

We notice in this passage that the presence of the Holy Spirit is identified with the presence of God. Where the Spirit is, there God is. The rhetorical question raised by the psalmist implies that there is no place a fugitive can reach that is apart from or outside of the presence of the Holy Spirit. The Holy Spirit is everywhere; He is omnipresent, ubiquitous. Again, such attributes are attributes that belong to the being of God and are not shared by creatures. Not even angels, spiritual beings that they are, have the ability to be present at more than one place at the same time. Although angels, including the fallen angel Satan, are spirits, they are finite spirits. They remain bound by space and time. They belong to the order of creatures. No created being is omnipresent.

The Holy Spirit is omniscient, omnipresent, and *eternal.* There never was a time when the Spirit of God did not exist. The Holy Spirit is also *omnipotent,* all-powerful. We notice in Scripture that the Spirit operates with special works that are the kind of works only God can perform. We see this both in the work of creation and in the work of redemption.

When we think of the work of creation, we normally think of it in terms of the activity of God the Father. Yet a close look at Scripture reveals that the work of creation is attributed to all three persons of the Godhead. In describing the preincarnate Christ, the Word, the *Logos,* John declares:

28

All things were made through Him, and without Him nothing was made that was made. (John 1:3)

Paul echoes this teaching of John when he writes:

For by Him all things were created that are in heaven and that are on earth, visible and invisible, whether thrones or dominions or principalities or powers. All things were created through Him and for Him. And He is before all things, and in Him all things consist. (Colossians 1:16-17)

Likewise the Bible includes the Holy Spirit in the work of creation:

In the beginning God created the heavens and the earth. The earth was without form and void; and darkness was on the face of the deep. And the Spirit of God was hovering over the face of the waters. (Genesis 1:1-2)

The Holy Spirit's activity in creation is mentioned or alluded to frequently in Scripture. The psalmist declares:

You send forth your Spirit, they are created; and You renew the face of the earth. (Psalm 104:30)

Job likewise declares:

The Spirit of God has made me, and the breath of the Almighty gives me life. (Job 33:4)

The Holy Spirit is the author of life and of human intelligence. (See Job 32:8; 35:11.) He is the power source for the conception of Jesus in the womb of Mary.

And the angel answered and said to her, "The Holy Spirit will come upon you, and the power of the Highest will overshadow you; therefore, also, that Holy One who is to be born will be called the Son of God." (Luke 1:35)

The Holy Spirit anointed prophets, judges, and kings with power from on high. He anointed Jesus for His ministry. In the New Testament the Holy Spirit is the power source for the resurrection of Christ from the dead.

But if the Spirit of Him who raised Jesus from the dead dwells in you, He who raised Christ from the dead will also give life to your mortal bodies through His Spirit who dwells in you. (Romans 8:11)

The Spirit exhibits power to effect things only God can do. In speaking of God's relationship to Abraham, Paul wrote:

(As it is written, "I have made you a father of many nations") in the presence of Him whom he believed, even God, who gives life to the dead and calls those things which do not exist as though they did. (Romans 4:17)

To bring life out of death and to create something out of nothing requires the omnipotent power of God. No creature can bring something out of nothing. No creature can bring life out of death. Nor can any creature quicken a soul that is spiritually moribund. All of these actions require the power of God. All of these things can be and are accomplished by the Holy Spirit.

The Holy Scriptures present the Holy Spirit to us as a proper object of worship. The Holy Spirit's inclusion in the New Testament formula for baptism is significant. John Calvin comments on this:

Paul connects together these three, God, Faith and Baptism, and reasons from the one to the other—viz., because there is one faith, he infers that there is one God; and because there is one baptism, he infers that there is one faith. Therefore, if by baptism we are initiated into the faith and worship of one God, we must of necessity believe that he into whose name we are baptized is the true God. And there cannot be a doubt that our Savior wished to testify, by a solemn rehearsal, that the perfect light of faith is now exhibited, when he said, "Go and teach all nations, baptizing them in the name of the Father, and of the Son, and of the Holy Spirit" (Matt. 28:19), since this is the same thing as to be baptized into the name of the one God, who has been fully manifested in the Father, the Son, and the Spirit. . . . What, then, is our Savior's meaning in commanding baptism to be administered in the name of the Father, and the Son, and the Holy Spirit, if it be not that we are to believe with one faith in the name of the Father, and the Son, and the Holy Spirit? But is this anything else than to declare that the Father, Son and Spirit, are one God? Wherefore, since it must be held certain that there is one God, not more than one, we conclude that the Word and Spirit are of the very essence of God. (Institutes I/XIII/16)

The Holy Spirit is included not only in the formula for baptism, but in the apostolic benediction as well:

The grace of the Lord Jesus Christ, and the love of God, and the communion of the Holy Spirit be with you all. Amen. (2 Corinthians 13:14)

We conclude then that the Bible clearly ascribes deity to the Holy Spirit. The Spirit is a person; the Spirit is God.

As soon as we make this dual affirmation we collide

31

instantly with one of the most important yet perplexing doctrines of the Christian faith—the Trinity.

How is it possible that we distinguish among three persons—Father, Son, and Holy Spirit—and still confess that we believe in *one* God? In the next chapter we will explore this difficult mystery of the Christian faith.

CHAPTER THREE

THE MYSTERY OF THE TRINITY

I bind unto myself today
The strong name of the Trinity,
By invocation of the same,
The Three in One and One in Three.

ST. PATRICK

NE of the best-known declarations of the Bible is the Great Commandment:

You shall love the LORD *your God with all your heart, with all your soul, and with all your might.* (Deuteronomy 6:5)

Jesus spoke of this commandment, saying,

This is the first and great commandment. And the second is like it: "You shall love your neighbor as yourself." On these two commandments hang all the Law and the Prophets." (Matthew 22:38-39)

When Jesus called the Great Commandment the "first" commandment, He did not mean first in the order of time. There were many commandments given by God before the Great Commandment was revealed. By "first" Jesus clearly meant first in order of importance. It is the law that sums up all other laws and upon which everything else in the Law and Prophets depends.

Before we can ever begin to love God with all of our heart, soul, and might, we must first have some concept of the God we are to love. There was a setting, a context, in which the Great Commandment was first given. This setting is called the *Shema* among Jewish people. The *Shema* was at the core of Jewish liturgy in the Old Testament. It was recited frequently in Jewish worship and was obviously well known by Jesus from His youth. The *Shema* introduces and prefaces the Great Commandment with these words:

Hear, O Israel: the LORD our God, the LORD is one!
(Deuteronomy 6:4)

The Lord is one! This confession of faith marks Israel as a nation absolutely committed to monotheism. Monotheism means belief in one God and only one God. It sharply divides Old Testament religious faith from any form of polytheism. Most ancient neighbors of Israel practiced polytheism. Their devotion was directed toward many gods and goddesses, even if they believed in a chief god. They had special deities for war, fertility, love, nature, and so on.

Normative for Israel, however, was the commitment to the unity of the one Almighty God. The First Commandment of the Decalogue (the Ten Commandments) reinforced this commandment:

You shall have no other gods before me. (Exodus 20:3)

This law totally excluded the worship of any other god or goddess besides Yahweh, the true God. The words *before Me* in the law did not mean "ahead of me in preference." That is, the First Commandment did not imply the idea that it was permissible for the Jews to worship and serve other deities as long as they did not rank ahead of Yahweh in terms of preference or status.

On the contrary, the "before Me" meant, "before My presence." What God was saying is that He would not tolerate the intrusion of the worship of any other deities at any place or at any time. To ascribe worship to anyone or anything apart from Yahweh was to degenerate to the level of idolatry and to incur the wrath of God for it.

It is because of this passionate commitment to monotheism in the Old Testament that the concept of the Trinity provokes so much consternation. If God is one, how can we justify the worship of three persons—Father, Son, and Holy Spirit?

The concept of the Trinity is designed to answer that question. The formula of the Trinity is this: "God is one in essence, three in person."

The formula seeks to protect Christianity from serious combat on two fronts. On the one hand, the church wants to maintain its strict adherence to monotheism. Hence the first part of the formula—"God is one in essence." This means simply that there is only one Being whom we call *God*.

On the other hand, the church seeks to be faithful to the clear biblical revelation of the deity of Christ and the deity of the Holy Spirit. Therefore the church distinguishes among three persons in the Godhead—Father, Son, and Holy Spirit. This accounts for the second part of the formula—"Three in person."

Before we attempt to probe more deeply into what this means, it may be helpful to deal with some common objections that are raised against the trinitarian formula.

OBJECTION 1: THE WORD *TRINITY* IS NOT A BIBLICAL WORD AND REPRESENTS THE INVASION OF FOREIGN PHILOSOPHY INTO BIBLICAL REVELATION.

John Calvin was particularly sensitive to this criticism. In replying to those who wanted to restrict and confine theological language to words found in Scripture, Calvin wrote:

If they call it a foreign *term, because it cannot be pointed out in Scripture in so many syllables, they certainly impose an unjust law—a law which would condemn every interpretation of Scripture that is not composed of other words of Scripture.* (Institutes, I/XIII/3)

What Calvin and other theologians have maintained is that the issue is not whether a particular word is borrowed from Scripture but whether the *concept* is biblical. We may use nonbiblical words in our theological expressions as long as they are communicating biblical concepts.

Calvin was acutely aware of the strengths and weaknesses of all human language. He wrote:

As our own thoughts respecting him are foolish, so our own language respecting him is absurd. Still, however, some medium must be observed. The unerring standard both of thinking and speaking must be derived from the Scriptures: by it all the thoughts of our own minds, and the words of our mouths, should be tested. (I/XIII/3)

The test of our concepts must be this: Are they validly derived from Scripture?

Orthodox Christianity asserts the incomprehensibility of God. By this I do not mean that we can know nothing about God. That which God reveals about Himself is understandable to an adequate degree. Yet there is a built-in weakness in our ability to grasp the things of God. No man can comprehend Him fully. Our knowledge of Him is far from exhaustive. Even the revelation of Himself that comes to us in Scripture is a kind of divine accommodation to our weaknesses. God speaks to us in our human language. Again Calvin comments on the Bible's frequent use of human forms to describe God.

For who is so devoid of intellect as not to understand that God, in so speaking, lisps with us as nurses are want to do with little children? Such modes of expression, therefore, do not so much express what kind of a being God is, as accommodate the knowledge of him to our feebleness. In doing so, he must, of course, stoop far below his proper height. (I/XIII/1)

There are compelling reasons why the church uses extrabiblical language to formulate biblical concepts. On the one hand, the church is forced to do so because heretics twist and distort biblical words to make them mean something other than what the Bible intended. It has always been the ploy of heretics to try and couch their doctrines in biblical language. Paul warns the Ephesians about this very thing:

Let no one deceive you with empty words, for because of these things the wrath of God comes upon the sons of disobedience. (Ephesians 5:6)

The "empty words" of which the Apostle writes are words that have been stripped of their meaning, drained of their genuine content. For centuries the church has had to battle against such misuse and abuse of language.

The purpose of technical theological language is to achieve precision of meaning as well as to safeguard the flock from cunning and subtle distortions of doctrine.

It has been said that it is impossible for anyone to write a creed or confession of faith that is so airtight that some unscrupulous persons can't redefine the terms to suit themselves.

A favorite tactic of heretics is to engage in theological quibbling over words. Calvin writes regarding this problem with the church's confession of the Trinity:

Such novelty (if novelty it should be called) becomes most requisite when the truth is to be maintained against calumniators who evade it by quibbling. Of this, we of the present day have too much experience in being constantly called upon to attack the enemies of pure and sound doctrine. These slippery snakes escape by their swift and tortuous windings if not strenuously pursued, and when caught, firmly held. Thus the early Christians, when harassed with the disputes which heresies produced, were forced to declare their sentiments in terms most scrupulously exact in order that no indirect subterfuges might remain to ungodly men, to whom ambiguity of expression was a kind of hiding place. (I/XIII/4)

Here we get to the heart of the matter historically. It was the Arian crisis of the fourth century that demonstrated so clearly the need for precise formulation of the doctrine of the Trinity. The chief "slippery snake" of the controversy was a priest by the name of Arius. Arius confessed that Christ was "God" and the "Son of God." However, under close scrutiny it was seen that Arius had redefined the word *God* so that it became virtually an empty term. The word *God* in Arius's vocabulary was ambiguous. Arius insisted that although Jesus was "God" by a process of divine adoption, He was nevertheless a created being. (If *God* no longer means *eternal Deity*, then *God* has become an empty word.) A profession of faith composed by Arius stated this clearly:

We acknowledge one God, Who is alone unbegotten, alone eternal, alone without beginning.[1]

The profession follows this with a long list of "alones," all of which emphasize Arius's view that the Son, or Word, is subordinate to the Father, who alone is the one God. God desired to create the world, and He brought the Son into being for this purpose. The Son is exalted, indeed, but is still, as Arius's followers never tired of pointing out, a *ktisis*, a creature. Yet because Arius continued to affirm that "the Son is God," earnest believers were puzzled. So the orthodox sought for a precise term that would indicate—with no ambiguity—that the Son was divine *and therefore coeternal with the Father and of the same substance with the Father.*

The theological term upon which Arius choked was a term borrowed from the language of Greek philosophy. It was the term *homoousios.* Never has a single theological term engendered as much controversy as *homoousios.* (The current controversy over the word *inerrancy* in regard to the Bible may prove to be just as dramatic as the earlier battles over *homoousios.*)

The term *homoousios* means "same substance" or "same essence." Arius was willing to say that Jesus was God. But he was not willing to say that Jesus was of the same essence (*homo-* means "same," *ousios* means "substance")

1. Quoted in J. N. D. Kelly, *Creeds in the Making* (London: Longmans, 1972), 232.

with the Father. The *homoousios* was the theological forked stick by which Arius's slippery neck was pinned to the ground.

However, Arius was willing to use the term *homoiousios* in place of *homoousios*. Note the *i* that follows the *homo*. Here the controversy began to turn not only on one word, but on a single letter. The subtle but crucial difference between the Greek *homoi* and *homo* is the difference between the words *like* (or *similar*) and *same*. *Homoiousios* means "like or similar essence," while *homoousios* means "same essence."

Arius appealed to an earlier verdict of church history when Sabellius, another heretic, had been condemned for using the term *homoousios*. Sabellius and his followers had been condemned for saying that Jesus was the same essence (*homoousios*) as the Father, so the church had insisted on the term *homoiousios*.

The plot thickens. This whole debate can become very confusing when we see that the church did an about-face with respect to which terms they allowed and which they condemned.

The reason why Sabellius had been condemned for using *homoousios* was because he meant something quite different from what the church in the fourth century meant by it. Sabellius's teaching was loaded with Gnostic concepts. Gnosticism was one of the earliest and most virulent heresies the early Christian church was forced to combat. One of its chief doctrines was a *modalistic* view of God.

In Gnostic modalism the universe was not seen as a

creation God made outside of Himself. Rather, the creation and everything in it was seen as a kind of extension of God's own being. All created reality is a kind of emanation that flows out from the core of God's being. The farther away from the core the emanations flow, the less perfect reality becomes. Spirit and mind are closer to the core, living matter is farther away, and inert matter (inorganic things such as minerals) is farthest away from the core. Still, everything that is is a *mode* of God's being and participates in His essence.

Sabellius said that the Son was *homoousios* with God but was not God. He was a close-by emanation from God, yet still removed from the core of the Divine essence. His analogy was this: Jesus was to the Father as sunbeams are to the sun. The rays of the sun are of the same essence of the sun. They radiate out from the sun, but they are not the sun itself.

Sabellius's concept of *homoousios* was thus condemned, and the church used the term *homoiousios* in its place. The reason for this word preference is clear. Sabellius used *homoousios* to show a *dissimilarity* between God and Jesus. Therefore the church chose the term *homoiousios* ("like essence") to declare its faith in the *similarity* between God and Jesus.

Arius reversed the situation. He used the term *homoiousios* to emphasize the *dissimilarity* between Jesus and God. He meant to say that though Jesus was indeed *like* God, He was not coessential with God. The fourth-century church said a resounding "No!" to Arius. The switch in terms indicated that the church was insisting that Jesus is not merely *like* God, but that He *is* God. He is *homoousios* (the same essence, coessential) with God, though not in the Gnostic sense.

The Arian controversy was not a tempest in a teapot, nor was it a game of theological shadowboxing. What was at stake here was the church's confession of the full deity of Jesus and of the Holy Spirit. It took an enormous crisis to provoke the church to change its preference of theological language. The Sabellian heresy had abated, and the new threat of Arianism was deemed so severe that it warranted the use of the admittedly risky term *homoousios* to combat it.

Though the church changed its choice of terms to express the deity of Christ and the Holy Spirit, the church did not change its concept. In both the Sabellian and the Arian controversies the church was using every linguistic tool at its disposal to insure adherence to the biblical concept of the Trinity. Far from seeking to circumvent or go beyond Scripture, the church was seeking to protect the biblical concept against those who would undermine it by the use of clever ambiguities.

The fruit of the Arian controversy was the Nicene Creed, which asserted the coessentiality of the Godhead and said of Jesus that He was "begotten not made," to disavow any hint of creatureliness in the Second Person of the Godhead.

The church hymn the *Gloria Patri* was also the fruit of the controversy. The *Gloria Patri* functioned as a trinitarian "fight song." The Arians circulated ribald and derogatory songs as part of their propaganda campaign against the trinitarians. In response, the trinitarians sang, with unified spirit, these words:

Glory be to the Father,
And to the Son,
And to the Holy Ghost.
As it was in the beginning,
Is now and ever shall be.
World without end.
Amen.

Here the Trinity is confessed in song by the ascription of a divine attribute—*glory*—to all three persons of the Godhead. At the same time the eternality of all three persons of the Trinity is confessed.

We see then that the term *Trinity* did not come about because the church was indulging itself in idle philosophical speculation or was flirting unnecessarily with Greek concepts. As Calvin insisted, the church was forced to use such terminology because of heretics who were subverting the biblical revelation concerning the Godhead.

The same type of controversy rages today concerning the nature of Scripture itself. Those who deny the full inspiration and revelatory character of the Bible will not hesitate to refer to the Bible as "the Word of God" or even as "infallible," yet they will choke on the theological term *inerrancy.* If indeed the Bible is the Word of God, infallible and inspired, why would anyone shrink from the word *inerrant*? Can something that is errant be the Word of God? Does God inspire error? Can something that is infallible actually fail?

J. I. Packer, an outspoken defender of inerrancy, calls the word *inerrancy* a shibboleth. As the difficult-to-pronounce word *shibboleth* functioned as a password to distinguish between true Israelites and spies (see Judges 12:6), so the term *inerrancy* functions in like manner. When the word is proposed to assert the full truthfulness of Scripture, the dogs begin to bark. To be sure, the word *inerrancy*, like the word *Trinity*, is capable of distortion and misunderstanding. But it functions well as a safeguard against those who have no scruples against using empty words.

OBJECTION 2: THE DOCTRINE OF THE TRINITY IS CONTRADICTORY AND THEREFORE IRRATIONAL.

I once met a professor of philosophy who complained to me about the blatant irrationality of Christianity. He said, "The whole structure of Christianity is built upon an obvious contradiction." When I inquired about what contradiction he had in mind, he immediately replied, "The Trinity!" He asked, "How can there be three gods and at the same time be only one God?"

I relate this anecdote for a purpose. Professional philosophers are well trained and usually highly skilled in the science and use of logic. It is their business to engage in close logical analysis of propositions. That such a professional would make such a bold attack against the church's formulation of the Trinity got my attention.

I am aware that many Christians would at least partly agree with the philosophy professor. They do not reject

Christianity as he did, but they agree the Trinity is contradictory. This doesn't bother such Christians because they are convinced that it is all right for Christianity to embrace contradictions because "God's ways are not our ways." Some even glory in contradictions, seeing in them the very sign of a higher order of truth. This is a tragic result of the form of theology known as Dialectical Theology or Neo-orthodoxy, made popular by such thinkers as Karl Barth and Emil Brunner. Barth insisted that one is not a mature Christian until he can embrace and live with contradictions. Brunner went so far as to declare that contradiction is the very hallmark of truth.

The idea of Christianity resting upon a contradiction may not bother the Dialectical Theologians, but it bothers me profoundly. In the Bible the contradiction is not the hallmark of the truth; it is the hallmark of the lie. It is the subtle tool of Satan. God said to Adam:

Of every tree of the garden you may freely eat; but of the tree of the knowledge of good and evil you shall not eat, for in the day that you eat of it you shall surely die. (Genesis 2:16-17)

"You shall surely die." This was the plain and simple assertion of God. "If you eat . . . you die." In logical terms this can be phrased: If you do *A*, *B* will inevitably follow.

Satan came and said, "You will not die." His idea was this: if you do *A*, non-*B* will follow. In other words, Satan came to Eve with a clear-cut contradiction. We can imagine the conversation running something like this:

Satan: Go ahead and eat, Eve, you will not die.

Eve: But, Mr. Snake, what you are saying is directly contradictory to what my God and Creator told me.

Satan: Eve! Don't worry about that. God's ways are not our ways. What may be contradictory to us is not contradictory to God. Besides, you know that contradictions are the hallmark of truth. Trust me. My contradiction proves that I'm coming to you with a higher truth.

Eve: It sounds enticing, Mr. Snake, and the fruit of the tree looks tasty, but I'm still not sure I ought to do this.

Satan: C'mon, Eve. Don't be naive. You're just hung up on Greek categories of thought. Are you mature or not? If you're really a mature believer you should be able to rest easy with contradictions. If you trust in my contradictions, you will not fall; you'll be making a great leap forward for mankind.

Eve: Oh, I get it. One small step toward the tree; one great leap forward for mankind. Let's eat!

Without the Law of Contradiction as a valid test for the truthfulness of a proposition, we have no way of distinguishing between righteousness and unrighteousness, between obedience and disobedience, between truth and falsehood, or between Christ and Antichrist.

The Law of Contradiction has no content. It provides no information. It is sterile, impotent with respect to its ability to furnish new knowledge. Its power lies in its force of government. It is like a policeman, whose siren begins to wail when we trespass over the boundaries of rationality. The Law of Contradiction is a firm master.

It tests our thinking for consistency and coherency. It abhors confusion and rejoices in clarity.

It has been said that "consistency is the hobgoblin of little minds." If that is true, then God is besieged by myriads of hobgoblins. His mind must be infinitesimally tiny.

God is consistent. God is coherent. In a word, God is rational. He is more than just Reason itself, of course. But He is—if we follow the Bible—a consistent Being. Those who favor a God of contradictions and inconsistencies must create their own God, for the true God will not suit them.

There is one aspect of Objection 2 with which I agree. The logic is valid at one point. If the concept of Trinity is contradictory, then the conclusion that it is therefore irrational would inevitably follow. I would even go farther. If it is irrational, then it is unworthy of our belief. God is not honored by nonsense statements. If our formula for the Trinity is contradictory, then it is a nonsense statement and ought to be abandoned.

The real question remains: Is the formula of the Trinity a contradiction? I could reply to my own question with a simple no. But that will not do. The answer must be more emphatic than a mere negation. I answer instead, "Absolutely not!" I put stress on the word *absolutely*. There isn't the tiniest shred of contradiction in the church's formula for the Trinity.

The rules of logic and the laws of immediate inference are objective and impersonal. They may be applied to propositions without emotional prejudice.

They are as unbiased as mathematical equations. When these strict rules are applied to the formula of the Trinity we see with absolute clarity that there is no contradiction in it.

Let us give the formula of the Trinity the benefit of the second glance.

God is one in essence, three in person.

The formula predicates two things about God, two different (though not contrary) things. On the one hand, it is predicated that God is one in essence. On the other hand, it is predicated that God is three in person. We can state it like this:

God is one in A; God is three in B.

Now if *A* and *B* are contradictories, then the formula would come closer to contradiction. If *B* is *contrary* to *A*, then we would call *B*, non-*A*. Then the formula would read:

God is one in A, God is three in non-A.

Even if this were the case (which it isn't), the formula would still not necessarily be contradictory. If a being or subject had four dimensions, we could say that the subject was one in *A* and also possessed three non-*A*s.

To sort this out we must review the formula for the Law of Contradiction (sometimes called the Law of Noncontradiction). The law states:

A cannot be A and non-A at the same time and in the same relationship.

This means simply that something cannot be what it

is and not be what it is at the same time and in the same relationship. Let me illustrate:

I am a man. As a man there are several things that can be predicated of me at the same time. I am a father, a son, and a husband. I am all three of these different things at the same time. But I am not all three of these things in the same relationship. I can be a father and a son at the same time but obviously not in the same relationship. I cannot be my own father. I can be my father's son and my son's father, but neither can I be my own father or my own son.

Let's return now to the formula of the Trinity. If we said that God was one in essence and only one in essence and then added that God was three in essence, we would have a bona fide contradiction. Something cannot be one *and* many at the same time and in the same relationship. So if we asserted that God was three in person and one in person at the same time and in the same relationship, we would be in the throes of contradiction.

But the formula does not assert such things. The formula says that God is one in one thing (essence) and three in another thing (persons). Unless it can be shown that essence and person are the same thing, the formula is not contradictory.

The distinction between essence and person was carefully drawn by the church to avoid making a contradictory statement about God.

The issue remains: is this distinction between essence and person a valid distinction? Is it merely a word game that poses a verbal distinction without any real difference?

We will probe this question in the next chapter. For now we conclude that if there is a real difference between essence and person, then the formula for the Trinity is neither contradictory nor irrational. It is logical and biblical.

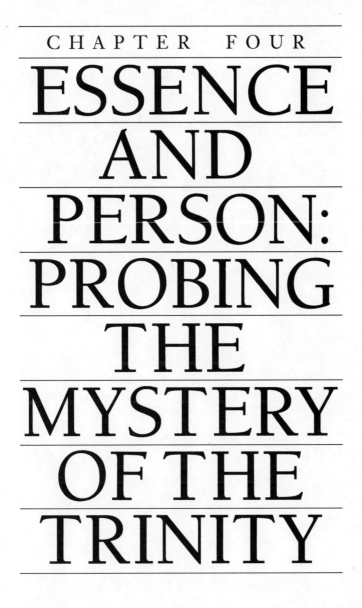

CHAPTER FOUR

ESSENCE AND PERSON: PROBING THE MYSTERY OF THE TRINITY

It does not take a great mind
to be a Christian,
but it takes all the mind
a man has.

RICHARD C. RAINES

BEFORE we analyze the distinction between essence and person that is so crucial to our understanding of the Trinity, we must first discuss the nature of mystery.

I have labored the point that God is not irrational. He is consistent and coherent. His Word is intelligible. But that does not mean that Christianity is without mystery.

In other words, I have distinguished among three thorny notions that are often easily confused with one another. These three concepts are *contradiction, paradox,* and *mystery.*

We have already given a definition for contradiction, so we proceed now with the other two.

PARADOX

The word *paradox* is sometimes used as a synonym for *contradiction.* This is unfortunate, as there is actually a clear distinction between the two words, a distinction that can be traced to the words' origins. The word *paradox* is made up of a prefix and a root. The prefix *para-* means "alongside of." We think of paramedics or paralegals, where the *para-* describes people who work alongside of the root subjects. But the critical feature of the word *paradox* is its root. The root *dox* has its origin in the Greek word *dokein,* which means "to think," "to seem," or "to appear." A paradox is something that, when it stands alongside something else, appears or seems to be the thing it is standing next to. A paradox is so-called because it *seems* like a contradiction. It looks like a contradiction. But it is not a contradiction.

A paradox can come so close to a contradiction that it can easily be mistaken for a contradiction. The formulation for Trinity is a genuine paradox. At first glance it may seem like a contradiction, but a closer scrutiny shows that it is not.

Remember the opening lines of Charles Dickens's *A Tale of Two Cities*? As a powerful literary device, Dickens made artistic use of the paradox:

It was the best of times, it was the worst of times.

How could the times be both best and worst at the same time? Only if considered in two different relationships. What Dickens was describing was a very real period of conflict in history when, in one sense, the best of times were experienced, while in another sense the worst of times were experienced. There was marvelous industrial expansion and, for some, the opportunity to amass great wealth. For them it was the best of times. For others there was an expansion of poverty and the increase of suffering. For those people it was the worst of times.

The distinction between paradox and contradiction grows more muddled with the introduction of a third term into the scene. It is the word *antinomy*. The word *antinomy* means simply something that is "against law" (*anti-nomos*). Originally *antinomy* functioned as a synonym for "contradiction" because an antinomy was a proposition or set of propositions that were against the Law of Contradiction.

As language evolved and underwent subtle changes, *antinomy* began to be used as a synonym for *paradox*. This is particularly true with the British use of the word. Now, when I hear someone use the word *antinomy*, I don't know for sure whether they are speaking of a contradiction or a paradox.

There is much in Christian thought that is paradoxical. Jesus was both man and God. The Bible says that we can only be free by becoming servants. These are paradoxes that are difficult to grasp but by no means contradictory.

MYSTERY

In its simplest form, the word *mystery* points to something that we do not understand. The fact that something is mysterious does not mean that it is not true. It is possible that with further information we will understand it, but for the present it eludes us. The Bible reminds us of this:

For now we see in a mirror, dimly, but then face to face. Now I know in part, but then I shall know just as I also am known. (1 Corinthians 13:12)

The Bible reveals many mysteries to us. For example, Paul writes:

Behold, I tell you a mystery: We shall not all sleep, but we shall all be changed—in a moment, in the twinkling of an eye, at the last trumpet. (1 Corinthians 15:51-52)

Again Paul writes:

> . . . *the mystery which has been hidden from ages and from generations, but now has been revealed to His saints. To them God willed to make known what are the riches of the glory of this mystery among the Gentiles: which is Christ in you, the hope of glory.* (Colossians 1:26-27)

There are mysteries that God has revealed. There are other mysteries that remain veiled to our understanding. When Paul speaks of the union of a man and a woman in marriage he adds:

> *This is a great mystery, but I speak concerning Christ and the church.* (Ephesians 5:32)

Recently someone asked me this question: "R.C., what makes light travel at a rate of 186,000 miles per second?" I was stumped. Perhaps physicists or astronomers can answer that question. I can't. I know light does travel at that speed, but I don't know *why* it does. I know that the essence of motion itself has baffled philosophers and scientists for millennia. There are many dimensions of reality that confound us, but our lack of understanding them makes them no less real.

Mystery is often confused with contradiction—for an obvious reason. Both are not presently understood. The difference is that a mystery may be understood with additional information, but a bona fide contradiction can never be understood. We cannot understand contradictions because they are *intrinsically unintelligible.* No one, no matter how brilliant, can ever understand a contradiction.

Now, I grant without reservation that the Trinity is a perplexing mystery. It is mysterious to us because we do not understand how one being can include three persons. We are accustomed to think of a ratio that equates one being with one person. Every individual person I know in this world is one distinct being. However, there is nothing in the pure concept of being that requires we limit such being to a single personality, simply because we are accustomed to thinking of one person as involving one being.

We run into the same type of mystery when we contemplate the person of Christ. With respect to Christ the church attributes two natures to one person. In Christ we meet one person who has a human nature and a divine nature. Again, this runs contrary to our accustomed frame of reference. The idea of one person with two distinct natures or essences is foreign to our experience. But there is no law of logic that requires that a single person cannot have two natures.

Again, we remember that one of the compelling reasons for the church's formulation of the Trinity in the first place was to fence the borders against heretics. The church had to guard on the one hand against tritheism (the idea of three gods, which is a form of polytheism) and on the other hand guard against forms of unitarianism, which would deny the deity of Christ and of the Holy Spirit.

The church established such boundaries at the Council of Chalcedon in 451. In declaring that Jesus was *vere homo* (truly man) and *vere deus* (truly God), the church was steering a course between views that denied the full deity of Christ and those that denied His true humanity.

When I was a student in seminary, a theology professor who later became Dean of Yale Divinity School made this comment: "Gentleman, if you want to go outside the borders of Chalcedon, you must decide to choose your heresy."

ESSENCE AND PERSON

In our formulation of the Trinity we have repeatedly spoken of a distinction between essence (or being) and person. Where did these terms come from? How are we to understand them when we apply them to God?

When we speak of the essence of God, we are borrowing a concept from Greek thought. It is the concept of *being*. Some theologians protest at this point. As we have already seen, this concept has been attacked as involving an intrusion of pagan philosophy into the purity of Hebrew thought.

It seems as if some theologians have more trouble with the Greek language than the Holy Spirit does. It pleased the Holy Spirit to use the vehicle of the Greek language as a means to convey the revelation that is the New Testament. In the New Testament Greek we frequently encounter various forms of the word *ousia*, which is the Greek word for "being." It is the present active participle of the verb "to be."

The concept of being is fundamental to the English language. I wonder how long we could speak or write without reverting to the use of some form of "to be." Words like *am*, *is*, *are*, *were*, *was*, and *shall* all have their roots in the concept of being. Being refers to what something is. When the ancient Greek philosopher Parmenides penned the profound words, "Whatever is, is," he was making a statement about being.

When we speak of the being of God or the essence of God, we are talking about what God is. We believe that God is His attributes. He is a simple, unified being in the sense that there are no component parts that, when added together, make up His being. God is not made up of two or more parts. He is essentially one. That is why the church insists in the tri-unity of God. The plurality of persons in the Godhead does not negate the essential unity of God. To think of the Trinity in terms of three parts of God is to fall into tritheism, by which the simplicity and unity of God are destroyed. At all costs the church has sought to insure that the integrity of biblical monotheism remains intact.

When the church speaks of three persons in the Godhead, it appeals to the Bible for support. There are some biblical texts that are crucial for this matter.

THE PROLOGUE OF JOHN'S GOSPEL

Central to the church's reflection upon the nature of Christ during the first three centuries of Christian history was the Prologue to the Gospel of John—John 1:1-18. John's use of the concept of *Logos* (*Word*) for Christ captivated the thinking of the theologians. Here we find the most abstract and perhaps the most profound teaching of the New Testament concerning Jesus.

John's Gospel begins with these words:

In the beginning was the Word, and the Word was with God, and the Word was God. He was in the beginning with God. (John 1:1-2)

These striking statements are made here by John about the Word (Greek *Logos*). The first is that the Word was "in the beginning." John goes on to declare that the Word was active in creation. "In the beginning" refers to the time of creation and indicates that the Word preexisted the creation of the world. That is, the Logos existed before the universe did. When theologians speak of the "preexistence" of Christ, this is what is meant. Normally Christian theology links preexistence with eternality. That is, in confessing the full deity of Christ, the church affirms that Jesus not only preexisted the world but preexisted it eternally.

Mormons and Jehovah's Witnesses agree that Jesus was preexistent, but deny that He was/is eternal. Since the Bible calls Christ the "First-born of all creation" and "begotten" of the Father, these groups argue that Jesus is the first creature created by the Father. Jesus then subsequently participated in the creation of the world.

John says more than that the Logos preexisted the world. He says that the Word was *with God*. There are two important aspects to this statement. First, we note the use of the word *with*. In the Greek language there are three words that may be translated by the English word *with*. There is the word *sun*, from which we derive the prefix *syn-* (as in *synthesis, synagogue, synchronize*). When we synchronize our watches, we match their times together with one another. The word *synagogue* uses this prefix to indicate a place where people gather together to be "with" each other.

The second Greek word is the word *meta*. This is usually translated to mean "with" in the sense of being "alongside of." When I walk down the street beside my wife, holding her hand, I am "with" her in the sense of *meta*.

The third word is the most intimate of the three. It is the Greek word *pros*. This little word serves as the basis of a larger word in Greek, *prosopon*, which means "face." The implied sense of *pros* is to be with someone in a face-to-face relationship. This is the word John uses in the Prologue. When John declares that the Logos was "with God" in the beginning, the idea is conveyed that the Logos enjoyed a close, intimate, personal relationship with God.

The second important feature of this statement is that here John clearly distinguishes between the Logos and God. This is a chief reason why we must make distinctions in the Godhead. The Bible clearly distinguishes among the Father, Son, and Holy Spirit. John 1 is Exhibit A of this distinction.

It is the third assertion of John, however, that most emphatically grabs our attention. He does not rest at saying merely that the Word was with God. He goes on to declare: "And the Word was God."

Here we find the clearest, most unambiguous assertion of the New Testament of the deity of Christ. Whereas in the previous statement John distinguished between the Logos and God, now he declares an identity between the Logos and God, using a form of the verb "to be." Here we see an identification of the being of the Logos and the being of God.

This is one major reason why the church in seeking to be faithful to the Bible has been compelled to insist upon a unity of being among the members of the Trinity. The Bible clearly declares an identity of being between the Logos and God. The two are one in being or essence.

Yet we still must honor the distinction that exists between the Logos and God. Two things are clear from this passage: 1. We must maintain the unity of being between the Logos and God. 2. We must distinguish between the Logos and God without doing violence to their essential unity. Though the two are distinguished, the distinction must not be an essential distinction or separation.

Mormons and Jehovah's Witnesses go through incredible linguistic gymnastics to evade the plain teaching of this text. Indeed, they torture the text to wrest their views out of it. For example, the Jehovah's Witnesses Bible translates the text in this manner:

And the Word was a god.

The justification used by the Witnesses is an erroneous linguistic one. In this text the definite article *the* is omitted. The Greek language has no indefinite article.

When a noun appears without the definite article, the indefinite article *a* may be supplied if the context warrants it. If ever a context prohibited such an insertion, it is the context of this verse. If Mormons and Jehovah's Witnesses want to insert the indefinite article *a* here, they slip to the lowest level of polytheism. If the Logos is "a" God, but not "the" God, we must ask the obvious question: How many Gods are there? If we know anything about the author of John's Gospel, we know that he was an unqualified monotheist.

Most Mormons and Jehovah's Witnesses would agree. They turn their defense to a more subtle line. They call attention to an obscure line from the lips of Jesus. In the context of a debate with His detractors the Jews said to Jesus:

"For a good work we do not stone You, but for blasphemy, and because You, being a Man, make Yourself God." Jesus answered them, "Is it not written in your law, 'I said, You are gods'? If He called them gods, to whom the word of God came (and the Scripture cannot be broken), do you say of Him whom the Father sanctified and sent into the world, 'You are blaspheming,' because I said, 'I am the Son of God'? If I do not do the works of My Father, do not believe Me; but if I do, though you do not believe Me, believe the works, that you may know and believe that the Father is in Me, and I in Him." (John 10:33-38)

The Mormons and Jehovah's Witnesses point to this text to justify the translation of John 1:1, "and the Word was a god." Here Jesus cites a reference from Psalm 82 in which the word *god* is used for mortals. So the

Mormons and Jehovah's Witnesses contend that for John to declare that the Logos was "a" god does not mean that John's purpose in the Prologue was to assert that the Logos was actually God.

If, however, we look closely at the text in John 10, we will see that in this exchange with the Jews who charged Jesus with blasphemy, Jesus was not denying His deity. Far from it. The text in fact involves a strong affirmation of His deity.

In this debate Jesus is responding to the charge of blasphemy. His enemies jumped on His claim to be the Son of God. They accused Him of blasphemy because "You, being a Man, make yourself God." Here the Jews at least understood what the Mormons and Jehovah's Witnesses fail to grasp—that Jesus did in fact claim to be God.

The subtlety of Jesus' reply must be understood in the context of the method of debate He employed. Here is a classic case of the *ad hominem* form of argument. In the *ad hominem* method one argues "to the man." That is, one adopts momentarily his opponents' position and takes it to its logical conclusion, demonstrating its absurdity. (This is also called the *reductio ad absurdum* form of argument.)

The Mormons and Jehovah's Witnesses interpret Jesus to be saying something like this: "You accuse me of blasphemy because I call myself the Son of God? Listen, I don't mean anything more than the psalmist meant. I am no more divine than those creatures who were called 'gods' in the Old Testament."

In this interpretation of John 10 Jesus would be escaping the charge of blasphemy on the grounds that the word *god* in and of itself does not necessarily mean Deity.

But this was not Jesus' point in the debate. The sense of Jesus' remarks rather is something like this: "If it was not blasphemy for the psalmist to say 'You are gods, and all of you are children of the Most High' (Psalm 82:6), then how much less blasphemous is it to use the word *God* to refer to the *only begotten* of the Father. That is, if in a minor sense all of the children of Israel were called children of God without blasphemy, how much less blasphemous is it to call the One who is uniquely the Son of God, *God.*"

In this same passage Jesus speaks of being sent into the world by His Father and then declares His unity with the Father: "The Father is in Me, and I in Him."

When we return to John 1:1 we see another compelling reason not to translate the verse "And the Word was a god." If we follow the reasoning of the Mormons and Jehovah's Witnesses, we would be driven to conclude that in one and the same breath John was guilty of the worst kind of equivocation in meaning. The logical fallacy of equivocation occurs when in the course of an argument or reasoning process the meaning of the terms in the premises *change.* John writes:

In the beginning was the Word, and the Word was with God, and the Word was God.

With or without the definite article, for John to reason

consistently, the word *God* must retain its meaning throughout the passage. If in the first premise the word *God* means God Himself, then, unless John equivocates, the same meaning must be applied in the second clause. If we follow the Mormon and Jehovah's Witness argument we would have to assign radically different meanings to the word *God* in one and the same sentence.

When we add to all of this that immediately following the statement John declares that all things were made through the Logos, there remains no doubt that John is identifying the Logos with the Creator God.

We conclude then that John 1:1 demands that we see both a distinction between the Logos and God in some manner and an identity between them in another manner.

HEBREW USE OF PERSON

When the trinitarian formula seeks to locate the distinction of the members of the Trinity in terms of person rather than essence, it looks to the Book of Hebrews for part of its rationale. The author of Hebrews writes:

God, who at various times and in different ways spoke in time past to the fathers by the prophets, has in these last days spoken to us by His Son, whom He has appointed heir of all things, through whom also He made the worlds; who being the brightness of His glory and the express image of His person, and upholding all things by the word of His power, when He had by Himself purged our sins, sat down at the right hand of the Majesty on high. (Hebrews 1:1-3)

Here the author of Hebrews describes Christ as "the

brightness of His glory and the express image of His person." We see a distinction between the person of the Father and the One who is the express image of that person. John Calvin comments on this text:

When the Apostle calls the Son of God "the express image of His person" (Hebrews 1:3), he undoubtedly does assign to the Father some subsistence in which he differs from the Son. (Institutes, I/XII/2)

PERSON, SUBSISTENCE, AND HYPOSTASIS

We notice in the quote from Calvin that he makes use of a technical word that we meet frequently in theological language. It is the word *subsistence*.

There are three words in the English language that have a close relationship one to the other, but which may be distinguished among themselves. These words are *essence*, *existence*, and *subsistence*.

One of the frequent questions I am asked by the laity is the question, What is existentialism? Everyone has heard the word *existentialism*, and most people have a kind of vague, shadowy feel for what it means. There is a mood of existentialism that has been widely communicated in literature, drama, motion pictures, and other art forms.

A key spokesman for existentialism in the twentieth century was the French author Jean-Paul Sartre, who died in 1980. Sartre coined a phrase that has become a sort of motto or catch-phrase for existentialism. His phrase, translated into English, is "Existence precedes essence." For our purposes here we can pass over the full philosophical import of this phrase. What is important for our immediate concern is that the phrase makes a sharp distinction between existence and essence, or between existence and being.

In our common manner of speaking we usually use the word *existence* interchangeably with the word *being.* We say that people exist and that God exists. We say that people are beings and that God is a being. We distinguish the being of God and the being of people by calling ourselves human beings and God the Supreme Being. We do this because we recognize that God is a higher order of being than we are. We are created beings. We are dependent, derived, finite, and changing beings. In a word, we are creatures. God is not a creature. He is uncreated, independent, underived, infinite and unchanging. But He is a being.

When we say that God "exists," we mean that He really and truly is. But there is a technical sense in which it is improper to say that God exists.

That may seem shocking. I am not in any way questioning the reality of God's being. But God's being is even higher than mere "existence."

The word *exist* comes from Latin words that mean, literally, "to stand out of" (*ex-*, "out of," plus *sistere*, "to stand"). What is it that existing things "stand out of"? Originally the concept was this: To exist is to stand out of being. It does not mean that to exist is to stand *all the way out* of being. If we were all the way out of being, we would not be. The only thing that is all the way out of being is nonbeing or nothingness.

To "stand out of" being means something like having one foot in being and the other foot in nonbeing. The whole point of this subtle distinction is to make room for creaturely being that is finite and changing. Our being is not *pure* being. Our being is mixed with becoming. We are both actual and potential. We are always changing. But God does not change. He has no potential. He is pure actuality. He is eternally what He is. As He said to Moses, "I AM WHO I AM."

The plot thickens (as if it were not thick enough already). The word *subsistence* makes another subtle distinction. To *subsist* means literally "to stand under" something. In theology it means not to stand *out of* being but to stand *under* being.

When John Calvin and other theologians speak of *persons* in the Trinity, they mean that in the Trinity we have *one essence (being) and three subsistences*. The three persons of the Godhead subsist in the divine essence.

The word *person* in the formulation of the Trinity is derived from the Latin *persona*. It is a combination of the prefix *per-* ("through") and the root *sono*. In the Roman theater a *persona* was a mask through which actors spoke. We have all seen the mask symbols that are the trademark of the theater world. There is the happy-faced mask that symbolizes comedy and the sad-faced mask that symbolizes tragedy.

There was a great struggle over the use of the word *persona* in theology because of its origin in the language of the theater. The Greek word that is found in the New Testament that is translated by the Latin *persona* and the

English *person* is *hypostasis*. Therefore, when speaking of the Trinity we speak of the "hypostatic union of the Godhead."

Commenting further on Hebrews 1, Calvin writes:

For the essence of God being simple and undivided, and contained in himself entire, in full perfection, without partition or diminution, it is improper, nay, ridiculous, to call it his express image (character). But because the Father, though distinguished by his own peculiar properties, has expressed himself wholly in the Son, he is said with perfect reason to have rendered his person (hypostasis) manifest in him. (I/XIII/2)

Referring to the verse where Hebrews describes Christ as the "brightness of His glory," Calvin states further:

The fair inference from the Apostle's words is that there is a proper subsistence (hypostasis) of the Father, which shines refulgent in the Son. From this, again, it is easy to infer that there is a subsistence (hypostasis) of the Son which distinguishes him from the Father. The same holds in the case of the Holy Spirit; for we will immediately prove both that he is God, and that he has a separate subsistence from the Father. This, moreover, is not a distinction of essence, which is were impious to multiply. If credit, then, is given to the Apostle's testimony, it follows that there are three persons (hypostases) in God. The Latins having used the word persona *to express the same thing as the Greek* hypostasis, *it betrays excessive fastidiousness and even perverseness to quarrel with the term. The most literal translation would be* subsistence. (*Institutes*, I/XIII/2)

We see then that when the Christian church confesses its faith in a triune God, it intends to convey the idea that there is one essence or being, not three, but that there are three distinctive subsisting personalities in the Godhead. The names Father, Son, and Holy Spirit indicate personal *distinctions* in the Godhead but not essential *divisions* in God.

I hope readers have stayed with the argument this far. More important, I hope they see its significance for a discussion of the Holy Spirit. Most believers would be happy to leave theological talk to the professional theologians and get on with living the Christian life. But centuries of theologizing have made it clear that the Christian life is not lived rightly without the right beliefs as the foundation. Not every Christian needs to be a seminary-trained theological scholar, but every Christian does need to understand the nature of the God we worship. (We are supposed to love God with all our *mind*.) Sometimes the understanding is easy, as when the sinner, seeing his need and seeing God's mercy, says with total sincerity, "Lord, be merciful to me, a sinner." But at times more headwork is required. And in the midst of many conflicting opinions and statements about God and the Holy Spirit, headwork is essential.

We could dispense with all the technical theology about the Trinity if we could all agree that the Father, the Son, and the Holy Spirit are one God, and yet that the Son is not the Father, nor the Spirit the Son, but that each has His unique subsistence.

In the plan of creation and redemption we speak of the *subordination* of certain persons in the Godhead to others. For example, though God the Son is coeternal and coessential with the Father, in the work of redemption it is the Father who *sends* the Son into the world. The Son does not send the Father. In like manner the Scripture says that the Son is begotten by the Father; the Father is not begotten by the Son.

Likewise we believe that the Holy Spirit is sent by and *proceeds* from the Father and the Son together. The Spirit doesn't send the Father or the Son. Nor does either the Son or the Father proceed from the Holy Spirit. In the work of redemption, as the Son is subordinate to the Father, so the Holy Spirit is subordinate to both the Father and the Son.

To be subordinate in the work of redemption, however, does not mean to be inferior. The Son and the Holy Spirit are equal with the Father and with each other in being, glory, dignity, power, and worth.

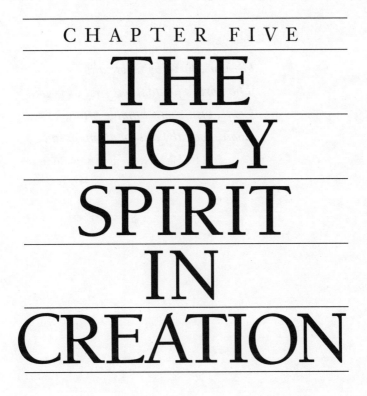

CHAPTER FIVE

THE HOLY SPIRIT IN CREATION

Creator Spirit, by whose aid
The world's foundations first were laid,
Come, visit every humble mind;
Come, pour thy joys on all mankind.

LATIN HYMN, "Veni Creator Spiritus"

THE CHURCH at Corinth was plagued by problems of disorder in the congregation. The gifts of the Holy Spirit, particularly that of speaking in tongues, were being abused and misused. What happened there may fairly be described as a charismatic free-for-all.

The apostle Paul wrote at least two major letters to the Corinthian church to provide pastoral guidance and admonishment. In his first epistle he labored the point, through three chapters, of the importance of exercising the use of spiritual gifts in an orderly fashion. He said,

Let all things be done decently and in order. (14:40)

I am a part of what is known as the Presbyterian-Reformed tradition. The cultural image of Presbyterians is that of staid, stuffy churchmen who furrow their brows at the slightest hint of spiritual spontaneity. One anecdote illustrates the point:

An alien came to earth and visited three churches. One was Methodist, the second was Baptist, and the third was Presbyterian. When he reported back to his superiors he said, "When I visited the Methodist church all I heard was 'Fire! Fire!' When I visited the Baptist church all I heard was 'Water! Water!' When I went to the Presbyterians all I heard was 'Order! Order!'"

Sometimes it seems as if the only text in 1 Corinthians ever read by Presbyterians is "Let all things be done decently and in order." There must be more to church life than order. Still, we cannot avoid the historical fact that the Corinthian church was troubled by a problem of disorder. The situation apparently was not rectified through the efforts of Paul's epistles. A later letter was sent to Corinth by Clement, bishop of Rome, who pleaded with the Corinthians to read again and obey the instructions of Paul.

In addressing the chaotic situation at Corinth, Paul made this important observation:

God is not the author of confusion. (1 Corinthians 14:33)

The apostolic statement is loaded with theological implications. We wonder what Paul had in mind when he set forth this overarching principle. His command that all things be done decently and in order obviously rested on this principle: disorder and chaos are out of keeping with the character of God. Disorder, chaos, disharmony, confusion—these are elements that are inconsistent with the character of God. These characteristics flow from fallen creatures, not from the Creator.

When Paul speaks of that which God authors and what God does not author, Paul was probably thinking here of God's way of acting in the original creation.

The creation story in Genesis 1 focuses on the triumph of God over any threat of chaos or confusion. At the heart of this consideration is the role of the Holy Spirit in creation.

The opening lines of Genesis record these words:

In the beginning God created the heavens and the earth. The earth was without form, and void; and darkness was on the face of the deep. And the Spirit of God was hovering over the face of the waters. (Genesis 1:1-2)

The first verse of Genesis reveals God's initial act of the creation of the universe. "In the beginning" must be taken in its absolute sense. This verse declares the mighty power of God in bringing the world into existence out of nothing (in Latin, *ex nihilo*). This is not a description of God's mere molding or shaping of preexistent matter. God's divine act was bringing something out of nothing, an action only God can perform.

When we use the word *creative* to describe the gifts and talents of human artists or musicians, we are using the term in, at best, an analogical sense. No human being has the power to be creative in the sense God is creative. All creative people use some already existing medium to display their creativity. A creative artist may shape things—words, musical notes, paints—in a new and striking way, but he does not work *ex nihilo*.

The Hebrew word Genesis uses for "create" is *bara*, which is used in the Old Testament exclusively in reference to God and His activity. It is never ascribed to human beings.

In the second verse of Genesis 1 we encounter a controversial passage:

The earth was without form, and void; and darkness was on the face of the deep.

What makes this verse controversial is the presence of three descriptive terms—*without form, void, darkness.* Think for a moment about the importance of these words. What do the concepts of *formlessness, emptiness,* and *darkness* conjure up in your mind? There is something very ominous about these words. We are threatened by these qualities.

Because of the ominous character of these terms, various theories have been propounded to explain their presence.

Critical scholars see in these words the presence of elements of myth in the Genesis narrative. Many ancient people saw the creation of the world in terms of a cosmic struggle between forces of darkness and forces of light. In Babylonian myth, creation resulted from a primordial struggle with chaos and sea monsters.

A relatively recent and widely popular view of Genesis 1:2 is the so-called Gap Theory or Restitution Hypothesis. In this view, only verse 1 of Genesis refers to the original act of divine creation. What follows after verse 1 is a description of God's redemptive restoration of an already fallen universe. That is, there is a massive time gap between verse 1 and verse 2—perhaps billions of years. In that time gap the fall of Lucifer and his angels occurred, as did the despoiling of the original universe.

A key consideration in this theory is the verb *was* in verse 2. Most translations of the Bible read, "And the earth *was* without form." The Gap Theorists have observed that the Hebrew verb found here may be linguistically rendered by the English word *became.* Therefore they render the text in this manner:

The earth became *without form and void.*

In this rendition verse 2 describes the disintegration of the universe into chaos as a result of sin.

The Gap Theory is attractive to many because it offers a viable explanation for the presence of the threatening terms *formlessness, emptiness,* and *darkness.* It also offers a way of escape for those who are convinced that the Book of Genesis reflects a life situation of relatively recent origin as opposed to scientific theories and evidence that the universe is billions of years old and man at least millions of years old.

The tension between science and religion has been intensified by Archbishop Ussher's attempt at dating the creation. By working mathematically from the genealogies presented in the Bible, Ussher, an Irish bishop living in the 1600s, calculated that the creation of the world occurred in 4004 B.C. (I have seen editions of the Bible that have printed this date in the top margin of the first page of Genesis.)

Despite the fact that the Bible offers neither a specific nor approximate date of creation, multitudes of Christians were reared with the teaching that the world was created in 4004 B.C. To defend that thesis against the assaults of modern science, they jumped on the Gap Theory bandwagon.

I am not persuaded of the truth of the Gap Theory. It has some serious weaknesses. First, though it is possible that the Hebrew verb in question may be translated *became* instead of *was,* the preponderant usage of the verb in the Old Testament highly favors *was.* Second, the theory smacks of an artificial contrivance born out of a dispute with science that, in my opinion, would not be necessary apart from Ussher-like speculations. Finally, I cannot believe that Genesis devotes only one verse to the crucial act of original creation and then abruptly, without warning or explanation, jumps over millions or billions of years of critically important cosmic events without mention of them. In other words, the plain sense of the opening verses of Genesis indicate a unified sequence of events that are tied together.

I favor the interpretation of the opening verses of Genesis as a description of the stages of creation whereby the elements of verse 2 describe the yet unordered and unfilled creation. It describes the condition of the earth in its initial stage before it reached its final state.

However we understand the first part of verse 2, we are still left with these questions: How did God perform His work of creation? What was the role of the Holy Spirit?

The only clue we get regarding the *how* of creation is found in verse 3:

Then God said, "Let there be light"; and there was light.

The power of creation is found in the power of God's command. Centuries ago Augustine wrote about creation. He declared that the source of God's creative power is found in the "Divine Imperative." He described creation as "fiat creation." The term *fiat* comes from the imperative form of the Latin "to be." God created the world out of the sheer force of His command. He spoke in the imperative—"Let there be!"—and there was.

This is what separates God's creative power from all creaturely creativity. No artist can paint a masterpiece by simply speaking to the canvas and paint, nor can he bring canvas and paint into being from nothing. No composer can create a symphony by simply yelling at woodwinds and brass.

How did Jesus raise Lazarus from the dead? He did not enter the tomb and administer CPR. He stood at a distance and called Lazarus back to life. Jesus uttered a command—a divine imperative—"Lazarus, come forth!" At the sound of Jesus' voice, brain waves were activated in Lazarus's skull. His heart began to pulse and blood began to flow anew in his veins. The cold, inert corpse began to stir, and Lazarus burst the cords of death. All of this by the sheer command of God Incarnate.

Hands and feet were not needed by God in His work of creation. There was no need of tools. He could move the world without the use of an Archimedean lever. His voice was sufficient. God spoke and it was accomplished. Something burst forth out of nothing.

THE BROODING SPIRIT

Added to the divine imperative, however, was the divine "brooding" of the Holy Spirit. Genesis says:

And the Spirit of God was hovering over the face of the waters. (1:2)

There is a question concerning the exact meaning of

the Hebrew word in Genesis 1:2 that is sometimes translated "hovering" and other times translated "brooding." The word occurs only two other times in the Old Testament. We find it in Jeremiah 23:9:

My heart within me is broken because of the prophets; all my bones shake.[emphasis added]

Here the word conveys the idea of shaking or trembling. Again we find the word in Deuteronomy 32:11:

As an eagle stirs up its nest, hovers *over its young, spreading out its wings, taking them up, carrying them on its wings* . . . [emphasis added]

When we think of the activity of a mother bird "brooding," we are inclined to think of her sitting on her eggs to keep them warm before the eggs hatch. In the imagery of Deuteronomy, however, the eggs have already hatched. G. C. Aalders comments,

The word brooding *just does not fit once the eggs have been hatched and the mother is involved in training her young. Thus it is more likely that the word here refers to the mother bird watching over her young as they learn to fly. When they falter in flight she swoops beneath them and rescues them from falling. When all is considered the translation "hovered" still has the preference.*[1]

Aalders continues in his explanation of this passage:

What then is the purpose of this hovering of the Spirit of God over the waters? It is obvious that it does not indicate a mere presence of the Holy Spirit. The purpose apparently

1. G. C. Aalders, *Genesis*, vol. 1 of the *Bible Student's Commentary*, trans. William Heyman (Grand Rapids: Zondervan, 1981), 56.

is that an active power goes forth from the Spirit of God to the earth substance that has already been created. This activity has a direct relationship to God's creative work. Perhaps we can say that the Spirit preserves this created material and prepares it for the further creative activity of God by which the then disordered world would become a well-ordered whole, as the further creative acts unfold.[2]

When we consider the full meaning of "create" (*bara*) in Genesis, we realize that what God creates, He also sustains, upholding all things by His power.

Creation is not a staccato work. It is, to use another musical term, *sostenuto*, sustained. We think of staccato notes in music as short, crisp, striking tones. Their duration is quick and terse. A sustained note lasts. It has endurance. It is never abrupt. A note on an organ can, in theory, last forever, so long as a key is being pressed. Creation is like such a note.

Part of the Spirit's work is to "hover" over creation, keeping things intact. In this regard we see the Spirit as the divine Preserver and the Protector. The Spirit works to maintain what the Father brings into being.

Most striking in the Genesis passage is the Spirit's role as *Orderer* of creation. The Spirit brings order out of disorder. His presence precludes the possibility of chaos or confusion. Here we see the Holy Spirit bringing *integrity* into the world. What I mean here by *integrity* is the structure of wholeness, the integration of the parts of the cosmos with the whole. It is because of Him that we have cosmos instead of chaos.

2. Ibid.

It is noteworthy that there is a clear parallel between the Spirit's work in creation and His work in redemption. As our Sanctifier He hovers over His children to produce integrity in their lives. He orders and preserves what God creates and redeems.

As the Spirit "hovers" over the waters, there is no more formlessness. The unstructured universe gains a marvelous structure. The intricacies of that structure become the focal point of scientific inquiry. It is because the universe is ordered and governed by coherent laws that science is even possible. Scientists could not do their work in an irregular and chaotic world.

Before the Spirit "hovers," the unfinished universe is marked by emptiness. Of the three descriptive terms of Genesis 2, perhaps this one is the most frightening to the soul of man. Human despair is often expressed in terms of a dreadful feeling of emptiness, a sense of the hollow, the threat of the void. In the darkest mood of the pessimistic existentialist we hear talk of the abyss, the Stygian darkness of the absolute void, the pit of nothingness. Even in human relationships we have a nagging sense of the threat of emptiness, which we identify with poignant loneliness.

The Holy Spirit fills what is empty. He conquers the void. When His work is finished, the once lonely universe is teeming with a plethora of flora and fauna. The barren wasteland becomes a pulsating arena of life. Here we need the Holy Spirit of God as the One who fills all things. Added then to His role of Former and Preserver is His role as the Filler of life.

THE SPIRIT AS ILLUMINATOR

But the Spirit does not cease His activity by forming what was formless and filling what was empty. When His work is finished, the primordial darkness is vanquished. As the Spirit hovers, God gives His first imperative: "Let there be light." And the lights come on.

The image of light in Scripture is crucial. It bears a marked contrast to forms of religious dualism. In some religions the metaphor expresses the images of light and darkness as equal and opposite forces locked in an eternal struggle for supremacy. There is no hope of final redemption where opposing forces are equally matched. The best that can happen is a tie. Redemption in such a scheme is an idle illusion.

In the Bible the power of darkness is no match for the power of light. There is no hint of a dualistic stalemate. The darkness must yield to the light.

I have always been intrigued by the power of light over the darkness. As a child I feared going down the steps into the cellar unless I first turned on the lights. I remember stepping into the awful hallway and standing terrified in the pitch blackness on the landing. I trembled as I groped for the light switch. My spirit was flooded with relief when my searching fingers found the switch and I pushed it. I didn't have to spend agonizing minutes to await the outcome of a battle between darkness and light. The instant I pressed the switch the frightening darkness vanished. The staircase was instantly bathed in light and I could descend the stairs with unflinching courage.

John put it this way:

In Him was life, and the life was the light of men. And the light shines in the darkness, and the darkness did not comprehend it. (John 1:4-5)

In the work of creation and of redemption the Holy Spirit functions as the divine *Illuminator.* The One who lights the heavens also inspires the Scripture, reveals God's Word, and illumines that Word for our understanding.

THE HOLY SPIRIT AS POWER SOURCE

When God creates life, He works through the Holy Spirit. At the ecumenical Council of Constantinople in A.D. 381, the church confessed and declared that the Holy Spirit is the "Life-giver" (*zoapoion*). The Spirit is the immediate source of all life.

We are accustomed to think that the only persons who "have" the Holy Spirit are regenerate believers. The believer is indwelt by the Holy Spirit and therefore has the Holy Spirit in a redemptive sense.

However, there is another sense in which all mankind, believers and unbelievers alike, "have" the Holy Spirit. In the sense of creation (as distinguished from redemption), everybody participates in the Holy Spirit. Since the Holy Spirit is the source and power supply of life itself, no one can live completely apart from the Holy Spirit. Paul declared to the Athenians:

. . . so that they should seek the Lord, in the hope that they might grope for Him and find Him, though He is not far

88

from each one of us; for in Him we live and move and have our being, as also some of your own poets have said, "For we are also His offspring." (Acts 17:27-28)

It is in God, through His Spirit, that we "live and move and have our being." Without the Holy Spirit there is no life, no motion, no being. The Spirit is the power supply for all of these things.

In the original account of the creation of human life we read:

And the LORD *God formed man of the dust of the ground, and breathed into his nostrils the breath of life; and man became a living being.* (Genesis 2:7)

We see in this passage that man receives life as a result of God "breathing" life into him. There is a play on the Hebrew word *ruach.* This word can be translated as "breath" or "spirit." The breath of life is inseparably bound to the Holy Spirit. It is by the Holy Spirit that men become living beings.

The Holy Spirit is also the life source for plants and animals. It is by the Spirit that the grass grows.

These all wait for You, that You may give them their food in due season. What You give them they gather in; You open your hand, they are filled with good. You hide your face, they are troubled; You take away their breath, they die and return to their dust. You send forth Your Spirit, they are created; and You renew the face of the earth. (Psalm 104:27-30)

Notice the activity of the Holy Spirit in the prophecy of Isaiah regarding the blossoming of the land.

...until the Spirit is poured upon us from on high, and the

wilderness becomes a fruitful field, and the fruitful field is counted as a forest. (Isaiah 32:15)

Job looks to the Holy Spirit as the Author of his life:

The Spirit of God has made me, and the breath of the Almighty gives me life. (Job 33:4)

The Holy Spirit is the power of life itself. In the New Testament the concept of power is closely linked to the Holy Spirit. The Greek word that is used frequently with reference to the power of the Holy Spirit is *dunamis,* power. We have two important English words that derive from the Greek *dunamis.* The first is the word *dynamite.* The second is more important for our consideration here. It is the word *dynamic.* When we use the word *dynamic,* we usually mean that which is "lively" and "active." It capsules the energy of life itself.

It is the Holy Spirit who supplies the dynamic for the created world. By His power the universe has life and motion.

As we have seen earlier, there is a parallel between the Spirit's work in creation and redemption. As He is the generating power of biological life, so is He the source and generating power of spiritual life. His work in redemption mirrors and supplements His work in creation. He works both in creation and re-creation of a fallen world.

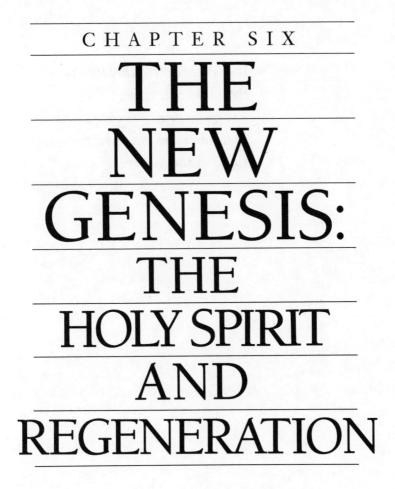

CHAPTER SIX

THE NEW GENESIS: THE HOLY SPIRIT AND REGENERATION

Without the presence of the Spirit
there is no conviction,
no regeneration, no sanctification,
no cleansing, no acceptable works. . . .
Life is in the quickening Spirit.

W. A. CRISWELL

BIRTH and rebirth. Both are the result of the operation of the Holy Spirit. Just as nothing can live biologically apart from the power of the Holy Spirit, so no man can come alive to God apart from the Spirit's work.

In His discourse with Nicodemus, Jesus said this about the Holy Spirit:

Most assuredly, I say to you, unless one is born again, he cannot see the kingdom of God. (John 3:3)

To be "born again" is to experience a second genesis. It is a new beginning, a fresh start in life. When something is started, we say that it is generated. If it is started again, it is regenerated. The Greek verb *geniauo* that is translated as "generate" means "to be," "to become," or "to happen." Regeneration by the Holy Spirit is a change. It is a radical change into a new kind of being.

To be regenerated does not mean that we are changed from a human being into a divine being. It does mean that we are changed from spiritually dead human beings into spiritually alive human beings.

Spiritually dead persons are incapable of seeing the kingdom of God. It is invisible to them, not because the kingdom itself is invisible, but because the spiritually dead are also spiritually blind.

REGENERATION AS NECESSARY

When Jesus uses the word *unless* in speaking to Nicodemus, He is stating what we call a *necessary condition*. A necessary condition is an absolute prerequisite for a desired result to take place. We cannot have fire without the presence of oxygen because oxygen is a necessary condition for fire.

In the jargon of Christianity people speak of "born again" Christians. Technically speaking, this phrase is redundant. If a person is not born again, if he is not regenerate, then he is not a Christian. He may be a member of a Christian church. He may profess to be a Christian. But unless a person is regenerate, he is not in Christ, and Christ is not in him.

The word *unless* makes regeneration a *sine qua non* of salvation. No regeneration, no eternal life. Without regeneration a person can neither see the kingdom nor enter the kingdom.

When Nicodemus was puzzled by Jesus' teaching he replied:

How can a man be born when he is old? Can he enter a second time into his mother's womb and be born? (John 3:4)

Nicodemus's response almost seems like an attempt to ridicule Jesus' teaching. In crass terms he suggests that Jesus must mean that a fully grown person must attempt the impossible task of returning to his mother's womb.

Nicodemus failed to distinguish biological birth from spiritual birth. He didn't differentiate between flesh and spirit. Jesus answered his response by saying,

Most assuredly, I say to you, unless one is born of the water

and the Spirit, he cannot enter the kingdom of God. That which is born of the flesh is flesh, and that which is born of the Spirit is spirit. Do not marvel that I said to you, "You must be born again." (John 3:5-7)

Again Jesus prefaces His words by saying, "Most assuredly, I say to you . . . " The "most assuredly"—the Hebrew *amen,* carried over into the New Testament—indicates strong emphasis. That is, when Jesus spoke of regeneration as a necessary condition for seeing and entering the kingdom of God, he stated this necessary condition emphatically. To argue against the need of rebirth to be a Christian, as many of our contemporaries frequently do, is to stand in clear opposition to the emphatic teaching of Christ.

The word *cannot* is also crucial to Jesus' teaching. It is a negative word that deals with ability or possibility. Without regeneration no one (universal negative) is able to enter the kingdom of God. There are no exceptions. It is impossible to enter God's kingdom without a rebirth.

No one is born a Christian. No one is born biologically into the kingdom of God. The first birth is one that is of the flesh. Flesh begets flesh. It cannot produce spirit.

Later in John's Gospel, Jesus adds this comment:

It is the Spirit who gives life; the flesh profits nothing. (John 6:23)

When Martin Luther was debating whether fallen man is utterly dependent upon the Holy Spirit for regeneration, he cited this text and added: "The flesh profits nothing. And that 'nothing' is not a 'little something.'"

The flesh is not merely weak with respect to the power of rebirth. It is utterly impotent. It has no power whatever to effect rebirth. It cannot aid or enhance the Spirit's work. All that the flesh yields is more flesh. It cannot yield an ounce of Spirit. The nothing is not a little something.

Finally Jesus says, "You *must* be born again." If there is the slightest ambiguity with the use of the conditional word *unless*, the ambiguity completely evaporates with the word *must*.

REGENERATION IN EPHESIANS

In his Letter to the Ephesians the apostle Paul speaks of the regenerating work of the Holy Spirit:

And you He made alive, who were dead in trespasses and sins, in which you once walked according to the course of this world, according to the prince of the power of the air, the spirit who now works in the sons of disobedience, among whom also we all once conducted ourselves in the lusts of our flesh, fulfilling the desires of the flesh and of the mind, and were by nature children of wrath, just as the others. But God, who is rich in mercy, because of His great love with which He loved us, even when we were dead in trespasses, made us alive together with Christ (by grace you have been saved). (Ephesians 2:1-5)

Paul provides a graphic description of our spiritual impotence prior to regeneration. He is addressing the

Ephesian believers and describing a prior condition in which they all once shared. He adds the phrase "just as the others" (2:3), presumably referring to the whole of mankind.

He declares that this prior condition was a state of death: "You were dead in trespasses and sins." Again, this death is obviously not a biological death, as he enumerates activities that these dead, persons were involved in.

The characteristic behavioral mode of people dead in trespasses and sins is described in terms of walking a particular course. He calls it the "course of this world" (2:1-2). Here the course of this world obviously refers to a course or pattern that is opposed to the course of heaven. The words *this world* refer not so much to a location as to a style or a point of reference. It involves a this-worldly orientation.

Christians and non-Christians alike share the same sphere of operations. We all live out our lives in this world. The regenerate person's course, however, is guided from above. He has his eye on heaven and his ear attuned to the King of heaven. The unregenerate person is earthbound. His ear is deaf to any word from heaven; his eye is blinded to the glory from on high. He lives as a walking cadaver in a spiritual graveyard.

The course of this world is "out of the way" of God (Romans 3:12). Rather, it follows a path that is "according to the prince of the power of the air, the spirit who now works in the sons of disobedience" (Ephesians 2:2).

The spiritually dead have a master. Their master sets

a course for them that they willingly—even eagerly—follow. This master is called the "prince of the power of the air." This sobriquet of royalty can only refer to Satan, the chief architect of all things diabolical. Paul calls him "the spirit who now works in the sons of disobedience." Satan is an evil spirit, a corrupt and fallen angel who exercises influence and authority over his captive hordes.

Paul sets forth a principle of life. We either walk according to the Holy Spirit or we walk according to the evil spirit. Augustine once compared man to a horse who is either ridden by Satan or by the Spirit of God.

Paul continues his vivid description of the regenerate person's prior unregenerate life-style:

Among whom also we all once conducted ourselves in the lusts of our flesh, fulfilling the desires of the flesh and of the mind. (2:3)

The attention now shifts away from the external course and the external influence of Satan to the internal state of the unregenerate person. Again we see this as a universal condition: "Among whom also we all once conducted ourselves . . ." The key descriptive word of this previous internal condition is the word *flesh*. Here Paul echoes the language Jesus used with Nicodemus.

The word *flesh* here must not be understood as a synonym for "physical body." Our bodies per se are not evil, since God made us as physical beings and became a human being Himself. The *flesh* refers to the sin nature, the entire fallen character of man.

98

Prior to regeneration we live exclusively in the flesh and by the flesh. Our conduct follows after the lusts of the flesh. That refers not exclusively to physical or sexual appetites but to a pattern of all sinful desires.

Paul caps this universal indictment of our fallen style by adding: "And were by nature children of wrath, just as the others" (2:3). When Paul speaks of "by nature," he refers to our state in which we enter this world. Biological birth is natural birth. Regeneration is a supernatural birth. Men were not originally created as children of wrath. Original nature was not fallen. Ever since the fall of Adam and Eve, however, the word *natural* refers to our state of innate sinfulness.

Every child who enters this world enters it in a corrupt state. David declared, "I was brought forth in iniquity, and in sin my mother conceived me" (Psalm 51:5). We are all spiritually stillborn. We are born dead in trespasses and sin. In theology we call this inherent sinful condition *original sin*. Original sin does not refer to the first sin of Adam and Eve; it refers to the consequences of that first sin, with the transmission of a corrupt nature to the entire human race.

We are by nature "children of wrath." How different this sounds from the socially acceptable notion that we are all naturally the children of God! This misguided idea is both long-standing and widespread. It is a falsehood that gains credibility by its frequent repetition. If you repeat a lie often enough, people will begin to believe it.

The lie of saying that we are by nature children of God

was a lie that distressed Jesus. He was forced to combat it and refute it in His debates with the Pharisees. The Pharisees raged under Jesus' criticism and said,

"We were not born of fornication; we have one Father— God." Jesus said to them, "If God were your Father, you would love Me, for I proceeded forth and came from God; nor have I come of Myself, but He sent Me. Why do you not understand My speech? Because you are not able to listen to My word. You are of your father the devil, and the desires of your father you want to do. . . . He who is of God hears God's words; therefore, you do not hear, because you are not of God." (John 8:41-47)

Although the Bible acknowledges that God is the Father of all men in the sense of His being the Creator of all men, there is a special sense in which the Fatherhood of God is defined not in terms of biology but in terms of ethics. *Obedience* is the operative word. In the biblical view, our father is the one we obey. The relationship is established not by biological ties, but by willing obedience.

Since the Pharisees obeyed Satan rather than God, Jesus said of them, "You are of your father the devil" (John 8:44).

In Ephesians 2 Paul speaks both of "children of wrath" (v. 3) and "sons of disobedience" (v. 2). These phrases describe all of us in our natural unregenerate state.

When Paul completes his description of our unregenerate state, he moves abruptly and gloriously into a doxology that praises God for His mercy. The transitional word is the single word upon which our eternal destinies depend. It is perhaps the most glorious word in Scripture, the single word that crystallizes the essence of the Gospel. It is the word *but*. This tiny conjunction shifts the mood of the entire passage. It is the link between the natural and the supernatural, between degeneration and regeneration:

But God, who is rich in mercy, because of His great love with which He loved us, even when we were dead in trespasses, made us alive together with Christ (by grace you have been saved), and raised us up together, and made us sit together in the heavenly places in Christ Jesus, that in ages to come He might show the exceeding riches of His grace in His kindness toward us in Christ Jesus. For by grace you have been saved through faith; and that not of yourselves; it is the gift of God, not of works, lest anyone should boast. For we are His workmanship, created in Christ Jesus for good works, which God prepared beforehand that we should walk in them. (Ephesians 2:4-10)

THE DIVINE INITIATIVE

Regeneration is the sovereign work of God the Holy Spirit. The initiative is with Him, not with ourselves. We notice that the accent with Paul falls on the work of God, not on the effort of man:

But God, who is rich in mercy . . .

We observe that the Apostle does not write:

But man, out of his goodness, inclines himself to God and raises himself to a new spiritual level.

One of the most dramatic moments in my life for the shaping of my theology took place in a seminary classroom.

101

One of my professors went to the blackboard and wrote these words in bold letters:

REGENERATION PRECEDES FAITH

These words were a shock to my system. I had entered seminary believing that the key work of man to effect rebirth was faith. I thought that we first had to believe in Christ in order to be born again. I use the words *in order* here for a reason. I was thinking in terms of steps that must be taken in a certain sequence to arrive at a destination. I had put faith at the beginning of the sequence. The order looked something like this:

Faith—rebirth—justification

In this scheme of things the initiative falls with us. To be sure, God had sent Jesus to die on the cross before I ever heard the gospel. But once God had done these things external to me, I thought the initiative for appropriating salvation was my job.

I hadn't thought the matter through very carefully. Nor had I listened carefully to Jesus' words to Nicodemus. I assumed that even though I was a sinner, a person born of the flesh and living in the flesh, I still had a little island of righteousness, a tiny deposit of spiritual power left within my soul to enable me to respond to the gospel on my own.

Perhaps I had been confused by the traditional teaching of the Roman Catholic church. Rome, and many other branches of Christendom, had taught that regeneration is gracious; it cannot happen apart from the help of God. No man has the power to raise himself from spiritual death. Divine assistance is needed and needed absolutely. This grace, according to Rome, comes in the form of what is called *prevenient grace*. "Prevenient" means that which comes before something else.

Rome adds to this prevenient grace the requirement that we must "cooperate with it and assent to it" before it can take hold in our hearts.

This concept of cooperation is at best a half-truth. It is true insofar that the faith that we exercise is our faith. God does not do the believing in Christ for us. When I respond to Christ, it is my response, my faith, my trust that is being exercised.

The issue, however, goes much deeper. The question still remains: Do I cooperate with God's grace before I am born again, or does the cooperation occur after I am born again?

Another way of asking this question is to ask if regeneration is monergistic or synergistic. Is it operative or cooperative? Is it effectual or dependent? Some of these words are theological terms that require further explanation.

MONERGISM AND SYNERGISM

A monergistic work is a work produced singly, by one person. The prefix *mono-* means one. The word *erg* refers to a unit of work. Words like *energy* are built upon this root. A synergistic work is one that involves cooperation between two or more persons or things. The prefix *syn-* means "together with."

I labor this distinction for a reason. It is fair to say that the whole debate between Rome and Martin Luther hung on this single point. At issue was this: Is regeneration a monergistic work of God, or is it a synergistic work that requires cooperation between man and God?

When my professor wrote "Regeneration precedes faith" on the blackboard, he was clearly siding with the monergistic answer. To be sure, after a person is regenerated, that person cooperates by exercising faith and trust. But the first step, the step of regeneration by which a person is quickened to spiritual life, is the work of God and of God alone. The initiative is with God, not with us.

The reason we do not cooperate with regenerating grace before it acts upon us and in us is because we cannot. We cannot because we are spiritually dead. We can no more assist the Holy Spirit in the quickening of our souls to spiritual life than Lazarus could help Jesus raise him from the dead.

It is probably true that the majority of professing Christians in the world today believe that the order of our salvation is this: Faith precedes regeneration. We are exhorted to *choose* to be born again. But telling a man to choose rebirth is like exhorting a corpse to choose resurrection. The exhortation falls upon deaf ears.

When I began to wrestle with the professor's argument, I was surprised to learn that his strange-sounding teaching was not a novel innovation to theology. I found the same teaching in Augustine, Martin Luther, John Calvin, Jonathan Edwards, and George Whitefield. I was astonished to find it even in the teaching of the great medieval Catholic theologian Thomas Aquinas.

That these giants of Christian history reached the same conclusion on this point made a tremendous impact on me. I was aware that they were neither individually nor collectively infallible. Each and all of them could be mistaken. But I was impressed. I was especially impressed by Thomas Aquinas.

Thomas Aquinas is regarded as the *Doctor Angelicus* of the Roman Catholic church. For centuries his theological teaching was accepted as official dogma by most Catholics. So he was the last person I expected to hold such a view of regeneration. Yet Aquinas insisted that regenerating grace is operative grace, not cooperative grace. Aquinas spoke of prevenient grace, but he spoke of a grace that comes before faith, which is the grace of regeneration.

The key phrase in Paul's Letter to the Ephesians on this matter is this:

. . . even when we were dead in trespasses, made us alive together with Christ (by grace you have been saved). (Ephesians 2:5)

Here Paul locates the time when regeneration occurs. It takes place when we were dead. With one thunderbolt of apostolic revelation all attempts to give the initiative in regeneration to man is smashed utterly and completely. Again, dead men do not cooperate with grace. The spiritually dead take no initiative. Unless regeneration takes place first, there is no possibility of faith.

This says nothing different from what Jesus said to Nicodemus. Unless a man is born again first, he cannot possibly see or enter the kingdom of God. If we believe that faith precedes regeneration, then we set our thinking and therefore ourselves in direct opposition not only to Augustine, Aquinas, Luther, Calvin, Edwards, and others, but we stand opposed to the teaching of Paul and of our Lord Himself.

REGENERATION IS GRACIOUS

In Paul's exposition of regeneration there is a strong accent on grace. It is necessary that Christians of all theological persuasions acknowledge willingly and joyfully that our salvation rests upon the foundation of grace.

During the Reformation the Protestants used two Latin phrases as battle cries: *sola scriptura* (Scripture alone) and *sola fide* (faith alone). They insisted that the supreme authority in the church under Christ is the Bible alone. They insisted that justification was by faith alone. Now Rome did not deny that the Bible has authority; it was the *sola* they choked on. Rome did not deny that justification involves faith; it was the *sola* that provoked them to condemn Luther.

There was a third battle cry during the Reformation. It was originally penned by Augustine more than a thousand years before Luther. It was the phrase *sola gratia*. This phrase asserts that our salvation rests on the grace of God alone. There is no mixture of human merit with it. Salvation is not a human achievement; it is a gracious gift of God. This formula is compromised by a synergistic view of regeneration.

It is not by accident that Paul adds to his teaching on regeneration that it is a gracious work of God. Let us look at it again:

But God who is rich in mercy, because of His great love with which He loved us, even when we were dead in trespasses, made us alive together with Christ (by grace you have been saved) . . . that in the ages to come He might show the exceeding riches of His grace in His kindness toward us in Christ Jesus. For by grace you have been saved through faith, and that not of yourselves; it is the gift of God, not of works, lest anyone should boast. For we are His workmanship, created in Christ Jesus for good works, which God prepared beforehand that we should walk in them. (Ephesians 2:4-10)

Have you ever second-guessed the Bible? I certainly have, to my great shame. I have often wondered, in the midst of theological disagreements, why the Bible does not speak more clearly on certain issues. Why, for example, doesn't the New Testament come right out and say we should or we shouldn't baptize infants?

On many such questions we are left to decide on the basis of inferences drawn from the Bible. When I am bewildered by such disagreements, I usually come back to this point: The trouble lies not with the Bible's lack of clarity; it lies with my lack of clear thinking about what the Bible teaches.

When it comes to regeneration and faith I wonder how Paul could have made it any more clear. I suppose he could have added the words to Ephesians 2, "Regeneration precedes faith." However, I honestly think that even that phrase wouldn't end the debate. There's nothing in that phrase that isn't already clearly spelled out by Paul in this text or by Jesus in John 3.

Why then, all the fuss? My guess is that it is because if we conclude that regeneration is by divine initiative, that regeneration is monergistic, that salvation is by grace alone, we cannot escape the glaring implication that leads us quickly and irresistibly to sovereign election.

As soon as the doctrine of election comes to the fore, there is a mad scramble to find a way to get faith in there before regeneration. In spite of all these attending difficulties, we meet the Apostle's teaching head-on:

For by grace you have been saved through faith, and that not of yourselves, it is the gift of God, not of works, lest anyone should boast. (Ephesians 2:8-9)

Here the Apostle teaches that the faith through which we are saved is a faith that comes to us by grace. Our faith is something we exercise by ourselves and in ourselves, but it is not *of* ourselves. It is a gift. It is not an achievement.

With the graciousness of the gift of faith as a fruit of regeneration, all boasting is excluded forever, save in the boasting of the exceeding riches of God's mercy. All man-centered views of salvation are excluded if we retain the *sola* in *sola gratia*. Therefore we ought never to grieve the Holy Spirit by taking credit to ourselves that belongs exclusively to Him.

REGENERATION IS EFFECTUAL

Within traditional forms of Arminian theology there are those who agree that regeneration precedes faith but insist that it doesn't always or necessarily *produce* faith. This view agrees that the initiative is with God; it is by grace, and regeneration is monergistic. The view is usually tied to some type of view of universal regeneration.

This idea is linked to the cross. It is argued by some that one of the universal benefits of the atonement of Christ is that all people are regenerated to the point that faith is now possible. The cross rescues all men from spiritual death in that now we have the power to cooperate or not cooperate with the offer of saving grace. Those who cooperate by exercising faith are justified. Those who do not exercise faith are born again but not converted. They are spiritually quickened and spiritually alive but remain in unbelief. Now they are able to see the kingdom and have the moral power to enter the kingdom, but they choose not to.

I call this view one of *ineffectual* or *dependent grace*. It is close to what Thomas Aquinas rejected as cooperative grace.

When I maintain that regeneration is effectual, I mean that it accomplishes its desired goal. It is effective. It gets the job done. We are made alive into faith. The gift is of faith which is truly given and takes root in our hearts.

Sometimes the phrase *effectual calling* is used as a synonym for regeneration. The word *calling* refers to something that happens inside of us, as distinguished from something that occurs outside of us.

When the gospel is preached audibly, sounds are emitted from the preacher's mouth. There is an outward call to faith and repentance. Anyone who is not deaf is capable of hearing the words with his ears. These words strike the auditory nerves of the regenerate and the unregenerate alike.

The unregenerate experience the outward call of the gospel. This outward call will not effect salvation unless the call is heard and embraced in faith. Effectual calling refers to the work of the Holy Spirit in regeneration. Here the call is within. The regenerate are called inwardly. Everyone who receives the inward call of regeneration responds in faith. Paul says this:

Moreover whom He predestined, these He also called; whom He called, these He also justified; and whom He justified, these He also glorified. (Romans 8:30)

This passage in Romans is elliptical. That is, it requires that we supply a word to it that is assumed by the text but not explicitly stated. The big question is, Which word do we supply—*some* or *all*? Let us try *some*:

Moreover, some *whom He predestined, these He also called;* some *whom He called, these He also justified; and* some *whom He justified, these He also glorified.*

To add the word *some* here is to torture the text. It would mean that some of the predestined never hear the call of the gospel. Some who are called never come to faith and justification. Some of the justified fail to be glorified. In this schema not only would calling not be effectual, but neither would predestination nor justification be effectual.

The implication of this text is that all who are predestined are likewise called. All who are called are justified, and all who are justified are glorified.

If that is the case, then we must distinguish between the outward call of the gospel, which may or may not be heeded, and the inward call of the Spirit, which is necessarily effectual. Why? If all the called are also justified, then all the called must exercise faith. Obviously not everyone who hears the external call of the gospel comes to faith and justification. But all who are effectually called do come to faith and justification. Here the call refers to the inward work of the Holy Spirit that is tied to regeneration.

Those whom the Holy Spirit makes alive most assuredly come to life. They see the kingdom; they embrace the kingdom; they enter the kingdom.

It is to the Holy Spirit of God that we are debtors for the grace of regeneration and faith. He is the Gift-giver, who while we were dead made us alive with Christ, to Christ, and in Christ. It is because of the Holy Spirit's merciful act of quickening that we sing *sola gratia* and *soli deo gloria*—to the glory of God alone.

CHAPTER SEVEN

SAFE AND SOUND BY THE HOLY SPIRIT

*To the one who remembers the Spirit
there is always a way out,
even in the wilderness with the devil.*

HERBERT F. BROKERING

THE THIRD PERSON of the Trinity is named the Holy Spirit. We wonder why the title *Holy* is ascribed in a special way to Him. The attribute of holiness belongs to the Father and to the Son as well. Yet we normally do not speak of the Trinity in terms of the Holy Father, the Holy Son, and the Holy Spirit.

Though the Spirit is no more and no less holy than the Father and the Son, the *Holy* in His name calls attention to the focal point of His work in the economy (plan) of redemption. The Holy Spirit is the Sanctifier. He is the One who applies the work of Christ to our lives by working in us to bring us to full conformity and the image of Christ.

In salvation we are not only saved from sin and damnation; we are saved unto holiness. The goal of redemption is holiness.

When Peter wrote concerning regeneration, he made this comment:

Blessed be the God and Father of our Lord Jesus Christ, who according to His abundant mercy has begotten us again to a living hope. (1 Peter 1:3)

We are newly begotten people, people vested with a hope for the future. In the light of this gracious work of re-creation and regeneration Peter adds this exhortation:

Therefore gird up the loins of your mind, be sober, and rest your hope fully upon the grace that is to be brought to you at the revelation of Jesus Christ; as obedient children, not

*conforming yourselves to the former lusts, as in your igno-
rance; but as He who called you is holy, you also be holy in
all your conduct, because it is written, "Be holy, for I am
holy."* (1 Peter 1:13-16)

Peter's exhortation begins with the word *therefore.*
This word signals a conclusion that is about to follow
based on the premises already set forth. In light of the
marvelous work of regeneration we are challenged to a
diligent pursuit of holiness.

What follows the word *therefore* is a strange-sounding
metaphor: "Gird up the loins of your *mind.*" We are not
accustomed to relating loins with mind. Peter's image is
reminiscent of Paul's panoply of the armor of God:

*Put on the whole armor of God, that you may be able to
stand against the wiles of the devil. For we do not wrestle
against flesh and blood, but against principalities, against
powers, against the rulers of the darkness of this age,
against spiritual hosts of wickedness in the heavenly places.
Therefore, take up the whole armor of God, that you may
be able to withstand in the evil day, and having done all, to
stand. Stand therefore, having girded your waist with
truth.* (Ephesians 6:11-14)

When Paul sounds the clarion call to battle, the first
preparation involves a girding of the waist. Peter speaks
of girding the mind. In His debate with Job, God
commanded Job to "Gird up your loins like a man" (Job
40:7).

The girding of the loins was the first act the ancient
soldier did to prepare himself for battle. The standard
attire of the day was the robe (in the case of the Roman,

the toga). The robe fell to ankle length for normal daily wear. When the bugle sounded for battle, the soldier hitched up his robe above the knees, securing its folds about the waist with a secure belt. This was the action of girding up the loins. If the loins were left ungirded the soldier could not move with agility. He would trip himself up in the folds of his robe. Once the loins were girded, the knees and legs were free to move swiftly and smoothly.

When Peter uses the image, he applies it to the mind. "Gird up the loins of your mind." This signifies that once the Christian is born again he must get ready for war. Entrance into the Christian life is entrance into cosmic warfare. The way of sanctification is the way of militance.

When I reflect upon my own pilgrimage as a Christian I cringe at the memory of hearing zealous preachers selling the gospel with a kind of Madison Avenue puff. I heard promises like, "Come to Jesus and all your problems will be over." "Have a simple faith and life will be simple for you." This may fly on Madison Avenue, but it will not work on the Via Dolorosa, the way of the Cross.

In one sense my life didn't begin to get complicated until I became a Christian. Before my conversion I was "at ease in Zion." I was comfortable in my sinful patterns. Life was a game. After my conversion I realized I was now playing for keeps. Every ethical decision was now loaded with moral importance. Now my conscience was alive to the Word of God, and I realized I was called to march to a different drummer than my friends and my society.

Though I was a small boy at the time, I carry some vivid memories of World War II. I recall those times when my father was promoted in rank. He started as a second lieutenant and was discharged as a major, one day short of colonel. When he was awarded a new rank he sent me his old brass and insignias. My mother let me adorn an army shirt with these items. (That's how I learned to sew.)

One of the insignia groups I got from my dad was hash marks. These single cloth stripes were worn on the sleeve to indicate years of service in the military. My father was not drafted. When the war broke out he was too old to be drafted. He was appointed as the head of the local draft board. After about two weeks of this service he shocked my mother by coming home in full uniform. He said to her, "I couldn't send those boys to war without going myself, so I enlisted." My dad entered the service early in 1942 and was discharged in late 1945 after the surrender of Japan. When he enlisted, he signed up *for the duration.*

When we enter the Christian life, we enlist for the duration. This war is not over in four years unless the Lord calls us home. The war lasts as long as we live. Each year we sew another hash mark to our sleeves.

To survive in this cosmic battle we need to gird up the loins of our minds. The battle with Satan is chiefly a battle for our minds. There is no greater folly, no greater peril to our sanctification than to succumb to the enticing seduction that says, "Christianity is strictly a matter of the heart."

God has made us in such a way that the heart is to follow the mind. God didn't send us a valentine to instruct us. The Spirit gave us a book with the content of revelation that we might be transformed through the renewing of our minds. Proverbs says, "For as he thinks in his heart, so is he" (23:7).

The author of Proverbs knew very well that the organ of thought is not the heart, but the mind. When he speaks of thinking in his heart, he is speaking of the deepest thoughts we have. We are what we think. Or perhaps it would be more accurate to say, "We become what we think." If our thoughts are constantly impure, the impurity will soon begin to show itself in our lives. If our thinking is confused, our lives will be muddled and chaotic.

In the process of sanctification the Spirit is our teacher. His textbook is the Bible. The Spirit seeks to inform our thinking. Repentance itself, the first fruit of regeneration, is a changing of the mind. Mindless Christianity is a contradiction in terms. Christians are exhorted to think—deeply—under the guidance of the Holy Spirit.

The Holy Spirit is also the Spirit of Truth. When Paul spoke of girding the loins and of the whole armor of God he said that the item we need for girding is truth:

Stand therefore, having girded your waist with truth. (Ephesians 6:14)

It is the truth that turns the spiritual soldier from a clumsy bumpkin into a swift and agile warrior. It is the truth that makes us free. Jesus put it this way:

If you abide in My word, you are My disciples indeed. And you shall know the truth, and the truth shall make you free." (John 8:31-32)

In His discourse in the upper room, Jesus promised to send the Holy Spirit. He said:

And I will pray the Father, and He will give you another Helper, that He may abide with you forever, even the Spirit of truth. (John 14:16-17)

Again He said:

But the Helper, the Holy Spirit, whom the Father will send in My name, He will teach you all things, and bring to your remembrance all things that I said to you. (John 14:26)

Perhaps the fullest expression Jesus gave to this concept is this:

Nevertheless I tell you the truth. It is to your advantage that I go away; for if I do not go away, the Helper will not come to you; but if I depart, I will send Him to you. And when He has come, He will convict the world of sin, and of righteousness, and of judgment: of sin, because they do not believe in Me; of righteousness, because I go to My Father and you see Me no more; of judgment, because the ruler of this world is judged. I still have many things to say to you, but you cannot bear them now. However, when He, the Spirit of truth, has come, He will guide you into all truth; for He will not speak on His own authority, but whatever He hears He will speak; and He will tell you things to come. He will glorify Me, for He will take of what is mine and declare it to you. (John 16:7-14)

In this discourse Jesus teaches His disciples much about the person and work of the Holy Spirit. He is called the Spirit of Truth. He is sent to us by both the Father and the Son. His mission includes fulfilling the role of our Teacher.

The Holy Spirit is the author of sacred Scripture. He is the One who inspired the original writings. He is the One who illumines the Word for our understanding. He is the One who uses the Word to bring us under conviction.

The Holy Spirit may be distinguished from the Word, but to separate the Word and the Spirit is spiritually fatal. The Holy Spirit teaches, leads, and speaks to us through the Word and with the Word, not apart from or against the Word. How grievous it is to the Holy Spirit when unbridled spirits mock God by claiming the leading of the Spirit when they are acting against the Word of God.

The Word of God is the Spirit's Word. The Spirit never teaches against the Word. The Word is truth; it is the Spirit's truth. The Word calls us to "test" the Spirits:

Beloved, do not believe every spirit, but test the spirits, whether they are of God; because many false prophets have gone out into the world. (1 John 4:1)

When we are called to test the spirits, the test concerns the issue of truth. The reason John gives for the need of such testing is because of false prophets. A false prophet is false because he does not speak the truth.

It is a classic mark of a false prophet that he claims to be speaking the truth. He claims to have the authorization of the Holy Spirit. These claims are fraudulent. Not everyone who claims to be led by the Spirit of God is, in fact, led by the Spirit of God. The Spirit is the Spirit of truth. He leads only to truth, never away from or against the truth.

Since the Scriptures are the revealed truth of the Holy Spirit, they function as the norm and test of truth. The Spirit does not contradict Himself. The Spirit is not the author of confusion. If someone alleges that he is led by the Spirit and then teaches against Scripture, he is clearly not being led by the Spirit.

The Spirit of Truth is the Holy Spirit. He instructs us in truth so that we may be holy. Learning the truth is not an end in itself; it is the means to the end of learning and practicing holiness.

It is not by accident that where Peter begins by calling us to gird up the loins of our minds he concludes with an allusion to the Old Testament mandate, "Be holy, for I am holy" (1 Peter 1:16).

SAFE AND SOUND

When the Holy Spirit regenerates us and quickens us to spiritual life, this action results in the awakening of the soul to saving faith. The fruit of this faith is justification. The moment we embrace Christ by faith, God declares us just. We are just, not because we have become instantly sanctified; we are just because the merits of Christ are imputed to our account. God counts us just in Christ, while in ourselves we are still polluted by sin.

Luther's famous formula to capture this idea is this: *Simul justus et peccator.* This phrase means, "at the same time just and sinner." We are just in Christ, through Christ and by Christ, while we are still struggling with our sin. Justification by faith alone means justification by Christ alone.

We see then that our justification *precedes* our sanctification. As regeneration precedes faith and faith precedes (logical priority) justification, so justification precedes sanctification.

However, it is absolutely crucial to understand and fix firmly in our minds that if regeneration is real it will always and ever yield faith. If faith is genuine it will always and ever yield justification. If our justification is authentic, it will always and ever yield sanctification. There can be no true justification without real sanctification following.

We must note at this point some critical differences between regeneration and sanctification. Regeneration is immediate and spontaneous. Our awareness of regeneration may come to us gradually, but the act itself, performed by the Holy Spirit, is instantaneous. No one is ever partially regenerate, or halfway reborn. A person is either regenerate, or unregenerate; there is no middle ground.

The same is true of justification. No one is ever partially justified. The instant saving faith is present, God immediately declares us just.

Sanctification is somewhat different. Though sanctification begins the moment we are justified, it is a gradual process. It continues as long as we live. Justification does not produce immediate full sanctification. Yet if there is no definite beginning of sanctification, that is proof positive that there was no justification, faith, or regeneration in the first place.

A second key difference between regeneration and sanctification involves the parties involved in their operation. Regeneration is monergistic. It is the work of God alone. But sanctification is synergistic. It involves the cooperation between the Holy Spirit and us:

Therefore, my beloved, as you have always obeyed, not as in my presence only, but now much more in my absence, work out your own salvation with fear and trembling; for it is God who works in you both to will and to do for His good pleasure. (Philippians 2:12-13)

This text offers the classic idea of synergism. We see two parties already involved in the working out of salvation. We are called to work, to work hard, with fear and trembling. At the same time we are promised that God is at work within us.

When the Holy Spirit regenerates us, He not only acts upon us and in us in a way that changes the disposition of our souls; He comes and dwells within us. As He indwells the believer, the Spirit continues to exert His influence upon us to assist us in our pursuit of holiness.

There is a danger signal at this point, a red light of caution that we must observe lest we fall into a serious heresy that is even now festering within the evangelical community.

When the Holy Spirit dwells in us, He does not become us. Nor are we in any way deified. Though I am now indwelt by a Divine Being, by the Holy Spirit of God, I myself do not become a new incarnation of God. There are those who are teaching even now that a person who is indwelt by the Holy Spirit is as much the incarnation of God as Christ was. This concept is so grossly heretical and blasphemous that I won't mention the names of these teachers here.

The Spirit works to produce sanctified human beings, not deified creatures. God does not make us eternal, self-existent creatures. God does not create another god. Whatever God creates is by definition a creature. What is created can be neither eternal nor self-existent. God could create an immortal creature, but not an eternal creature. An immortal creature would have the ability to live forever into the future but not eternally in the past.

When God the Holy Spirit quickens us to the faith by which we are justified, we are safe. Justification saves us from the wrath that is to come. At the moment of our justification, as Martin Luther's formula indicated, we are safe, but not sound. Luther made the further analogy that the physician has declared that we will most certainly live even though the illness has not yet been

125

healed. But with sanctifying grace we are given the medicine that will restore us fully.

O. P. Gifford offered the following illustration to describe the process of sanctification:

The steamship whose machinery is broken may be brought into port and made fast to the dock. She is safe, but not sound. Repairs may last a long time. Christ designs to make us both safe and sound. Justification gives the first—safety; sanctification gives the second—soundness.[1]

In our day there is a dispute among Christians about the possibility of embracing Christ as Savior while not embracing Him as Lord. This Savior/Lord dichotomy is as far from the biblical concept of justification-sanctification as we can stray. A. A. Hodge once remarked, "Any man who thinks he is a Christian, and that he has accepted Christ for sanctification, is miserably deluded in that very experience."[2]

There can be no justifying faith that receives Jesus as Savior while at the same time ignores, rejects, or passes Him over as Lord. Though we can distinguish between the roles Jesus performs as Savior and Lord, we can by no means separate them. To embrace Christ by faith is to embrace the whole Christ.

Again, as we distinguish between the Holy Spirit's work in regeneration and sanctification there remains a necessary connection between the two. We are regenerated into faith, unto justification, and unto sanctification.

1. A. H. Strong, *Systematic Theology* (Old Tappan, N. J.: Fleming H. Revell, 1907), 869.
2. Ibid.

A. H. Strong writes:

The operation of God reveals itself in, and is accompanied by, intelligent and voluntary activity of the believer in the discovery and mortification of sinful desires, and in the bringing of the whole being into obedience to Christ and conformity to the standards of His Word.[3]

Sanctification involves movement. We usually refer to that movement in terms of spiritual growth. At times it may seem as if we are taking two steps forward and one step backward. We speak of "backsliding" as we slip and fall in our spiritual walk. Yet the overall pattern of sanctification is one of growth. The growth is gradual; it may be painfully slow at times. But there must be movement. Again, no Christian is spiritually stillborn. Strong cites Horace Bushnell in this regard:

If the stars did not move, they would rot in the sky. The man who rides the bicycle must either go on, or go off. A large part of sanctification consists in the formation of proper habits, such as the habit of Scripture reading, of secret prayer, of church going, of efforts to convert and bene- fit others.[4]

I like Bushnell's bicycle analogy. To maintain balance on a bicycle one must keep the bike in motion. As soon as the bicycle's momentum stops we better have long enough legs to reach the ground or we will surely fall. I learned to ride a bicycle while my legs were still too short to reach the ground when the bike was stationary. I set a mattress on the driveway by my stopping place to insure that when I came to a stop I had a soft place upon which to fall.

3. Ibid., 871.
4. Ibid., 872.

127

THE ROLE OF THE CONSCIENCE
IN SANCTIFICATION

The changes sanctification brings to our lives work from the inside out. Our outward behaviors manifest the inward disposition of our heart and the thinking of our minds.

There are three important changes that are wrought in us by the Holy Spirit as He works upon our minds and our hearts.

There is a change in our consciousness. The Spirit awakens within us a new awareness. As we listen attentively to the Word of God we become aware of the things of God in a new way. As we are born again, behold, all things become new. We gain spiritual discernment:

Now we have received, not the spirit of the world, but the Spirit who is from God, that we might know the things that have been freely given to us by God. These things we also speak, not in words which man's wisdom teaches but which the Holy Spirit teaches, comparing spiritual things with spiritual. But the natural man does not receive the things of the Spirit of God, for they are foolishness to him; nor can he know them, because they are spiritually discerned. But he who is spiritual judges all things, yet he himself is rightly judged by no one. For "who has known the mind of the Lord that he may instruct Him?" But we have the mind of Christ. (1 Corinthians 2:12-16)

To have the mind of Christ is to think as He does. It is to affirm what He affirms and to deny what He denies. It is to love what He loves and to hate what He hates.

Our sanctification begins to take hold when our thinking changes. We become aware of a new perspective, a whole new value system.

But it is not enough for us to be merely conscious of the truth. For us to *do* the truth, that consciousness must involve an intensity level that we call conviction.

The Holy Spirit works not only to give us an awareness of the truth; He works to convince us of the truth. He convicts us of sin and of righteousness. I may think or passively realize, for example, that it is wrong to steal. Yet if that realization is vague and weak in my mind it is unlikely that my behavior will change.

For every truth that God reveals there is a corresponding lie that attacks it. We may realize that fornication is a sin. Yet the voices of our culture so loudly and persistently proclaim that it is normal and OK that our resolve for chastity is weakened. We must be firmly and thoroughly convinced of the sinfulness of sin if we are to avoid the seductions of our culture.

Behavior change becomes dramatic when we pass through the stages of awareness to conviction and reach the point where our consciences are changed.

The conscience of man is a powerful but changeable mechanism. It has been called the "internal voice of God," a kind of built-in governor that either accuses or excuses us. The conscience serves as a monitor of our behavior. The problem with our conscience is that it may be acutely sensitive to the Word of God or it may be desensitized.

As sinners we are adept at searing our consciences. We are masters of rationalization by which we mute the accusing sound of the inner voice.

There are people who argue furiously that abortion is a monstrous evil, while others claim it is morally justifiable. The person who cheats in school or at work has an intricately conceived self-justification for it. Surely Hitler provided a moral justification for his actions in the Holocaust. Few people say forthrightly, "What I'm doing is evil, but I'm doing it anyway because I enjoy it."

We may admit that certain actions are sinful, but we insist the sin in them is minor and inconsequential. We may even add the catch-all excuse, "At least I'm honest about what I'm doing," as if an honest admission to a crime excuses the crime.

It is a rare thing for us to ever recognize or acknowledge the gravity of our sin. Our confessions of sin tend to lack deep conviction.

God spoke through the prophet Jeremiah to rebuke Israel for being to herself:

Yet you say, "Because I am innocent, surely His anger shall turn from me." Behold, I will plead my case against you, because you say, "I have not sinned." (Jeremiah 2:35)

Jeremiah compared Israel to one who has "a harlot's forehead; you refuse to be ashamed" (3:3). Like the harlot, Israel, through constant and repeated sin, lost her ability to blush.

Israel's sin reveals the deadly result of a seared conscience. She grew comfortable with her sin to the point that she could sin and no longer feel guilty. She had effectively silenced the voice of conscience. Her conscience began to work to excuse her when it should have accused her.

A good conscience is one trained by the Holy Spirit through the Word of God. When we understand God's truth clearly and are convicted by it firmly, then the governor of conscience begins to rule us into righteousness. The spiritually mature conscience is scrupulous. It does not allow what the flesh allows.

The Christian conscience is to be alive to the Word of God. It is no tyrant that paralyzes us with morbid guilt. If it is trained by the Word of God it will be healthy. We will feel guilt when we are truly guilty. That is as essential to spiritual health as real pain is to physical health. Pain signals illness. If we lose the capacity to experience pain we have no alert system to serious illness.

Jiminy Cricket told Pinocchio, "Always let your conscience be your guide." That is fatal advice if the conscience is seared and out of harmony with the Word of God. Yet it is sound advice if, like Luther, our consciences are held captive by the Word of God.

From consciousness of the Word of God, the Spirit moves us to conviction of the Word of God. From conviction the Spirit redeems our consciences that we may be conformed to the image of Christ. This is the goal of sanctification, the end point toward which the Spirit strives within us.

CHAPTER EIGHT

THE BAPTISM OF THE HOLY SPIRIT

*The Spirit-filled life is no mystery
revealed to a select few,
no goal difficult of attainment.
To trust and obey is the substance
of the whole matter.*

V. RAYMOND EDMAN

ONE of the most spectacular movements ever to sweep through the Christian church is the Charismatic movement. From the outbreak of speaking in tongues in the Azusa Street Mission in Los Angeles in the early part of the twentieth century to the growth of the Pentecostal and Assemblies of God churches to the spread into the Roman Catholic church and mainline Protestant churches in the 1960s, the charismatic revival has sparked zealous devotion among its adherents and fueled deep theological discussion. No church historian can ignore the impact of Charismatics on the modern church.

Christian television broadcasting has been dominated by Charismatic programming, as seen on "The 700 Club," the Trinity Broadcasting Network, and (formerly) the PTL network. Pat Robertson's bid for the presidency of the United States in 1988 revealed in part the enormous following that Charismatic Christianity has enjoyed. The scandals that rocked the church focusing on the misdeeds of Jim Bakker and Jimmy Swaggart have not dampened the zeal that attends the broader Charismatic revival.

It is not within the scope of this book to chronicle the history of the Charismatic movement or to evaluate in detail all the dimensions of Charismatic theology. Many books have already been written on the subject.[1] My

1. For an excellent historical summary and analysis see *A Theology of the Holy Spirit* by Frederick Dale Bruner (Grand Rapids: Eerdmans, 1970).

focal point in this chapter will be on one central doctrine that is at the core of Charismatic/Neo-Pentecostal theology: the baptism of the Holy Spirit.

THE DOCTRINE OF THE BAPTISM OF THE HOLY SPIRIT

Before I summarize the Neo-Pentecostal view of the baptism of the Holy Spirit, we must first note the historic rationale for using the prefix *Neo-* with the root *Pentecostal.*

Neo-Pentecostalism refers to a significant modification in teaching with respect to classical Pentecostal theology. The "Neo-" or "New" Pentecostalism has a far broader base than merely being located in the Pentecostal church as such. In the original Pentecostal denominations the baptism of the Holy Spirit was linked to a concept of sanctification that was integral to the so-called Holiness movement.

As we've seen earlier, the Holiness movement stressed the idea of sanctification as a second work of grace (following regeneration) that was instantaneous and produced either complete or partial moral perfection. Though the term *partial perfectionism* sounds strange to the ear, it involves some important distinctions. Indeed, partial perfectionism implies partial *imperfectionism,* which tends to cloud the whole idea of perfectionism. Strictly speaking, that which is perfect allows for no mars, blemishes, or other types of imperfections.

Some perfectionists argued that the second work of grace achieved total, pure, and complete sanctification, whereby the recipient was altogether free of sin. John Wesley, in his version of perfectionism, stopped short of this and restricted perfectionism to the reception of the spiritual power of a perfected love. The hymn "O Perfect Love," which ironically is used often in weddings, had its origin in an expression of this Wesleyan doctrine of sanctification.

Other Holiness advocates have modified the view of the "second blessing" to restrict it to achieving a victorious life over "willful sin." That is, once a person receives the baptism of the Holy Spirit into sanctification, he may still sin, but never willfully. Whatever sin remains in the sanctified person is accidental sin or sin committed in ignorance. The baptism of the Holy Spirit so sanctifies a person that he is then free of deliberate sin.

Though some churches still teach such perfectionistic doctrines, the idea of perfectionism either in whole or in part has not made many inroads into mainstream Christianity. The tendency in such theology is to either diminish the rigorous demands of God's law or to inflate the individual's own sense of spiritual achievement. For a person to remain convinced that he is living without sin, he must avoid either a close scrutiny of God's law or a close and honest scrutiny of his own performance.

The evidence of continued sin in the lives of the greatest saints is so strong that it is virtually inevitable that forms of perfectionism tend to be modified, limited, and restricted to some degree of partial perfectionism, which, of course, is but another term for imperfectionism.

In Neo-Pentecostal theology the link between moral perfectionism and the baptism of the Holy Spirit has all but been abandoned. We do not hear Charismatic leaders such as Pat Robertson speaking of being totally sanctified. And Jim Bakker makes no claims to being perfect.

In Neo-Pentecostal theology the emphasis on the baptism of the Holy Spirit falls upon the idea of being *empowered* or *gifted* for *ministry*. The word *charismatic* itself derives from the New Testament Greek word for "gift" or "spiritual grace." The English word *charismatic* has become so widely used that it has found its way into the lexicon of popular speech. An exciting performer or political leader may be called "charismatic" without any religious overtones connected to the word.

Since the Neo-Pentecostal movement has penetrated virtually all of the Christian denominations, its theology has been shaped by the theologies of the various churches. For example, Roman Catholic Charismatics have a Roman Catholic flavor to their theology, just as Lutheran and Episcopalian Charismatics have their distinctive flavors.

Since Neo-Pentecostalism has touched so many traditions, it is not surprising that no monolithic Neo-Pentecostal theology has emerged from the movement. This makes it necessary to speak in general terms and point to overall trends in the movement.

The basic trend in Neo-Pentecostal theology is to see the baptism of the Holy Spirit as a special work of the Holy Spirit by which a believer is endued with power for life and service. He is now gifted for ministry. This work of the Holy Spirit is distinct from, and usually subsequent to, the Spirit's work of regeneration. Sometimes a distinction is made between being baptized "by" or "of" the Holy Spirit (which occurs at rebirth) and baptism "in" or "with" the Holy Spirit (which normally follows *after* rebirth). In this schema all Christians are baptized "by" the Spirit, but not all Christians are baptized "in" or "with" the Spirit.

Though there is widespread disagreement among Neo-Pentecostals on this point, the trend is to see speaking in tongues (glossolalia) as the initial evidence of Holy Spirit baptism.

PENTECOSTALISM AND PENTECOST

Pentecostalism derives its name from its emphasis upon its understanding of what happened to the church on the Day of Pentecost. The record of the Holy Spirit's activity in the life of the early church is pivotal for the modern Charismatic movement. There is a strong desire to recapture the spiritual power and vitality evinced in the Book of Acts:

Now when the Day of Pentecost had fully come, they were all with one accord in one place. And suddenly there came a sound from heaven, as of a rushing mighty wind, and it filled the whole house where they were sitting. Then there appeared to them divided tongues, as of fire, and one sat upon each of them. And they were all filled with the Holy Spirit and began to speak with other tongues, as the Spirit gave them utterance. (Acts 2:1-4)

139

Later in the record Peter speaks to the perplexed observers of this phenomenon and offers this interpretation of the event:

These are not drunk, as you suppose, since it is only the third hour of the day. But this is what was spoken by the prophet Joel: "And it shall come to pass in the last days, says God, that I will pour out of My Spirit on all flesh." (Acts 2:15-17)

Toward the end of Peter's sermon he makes this observation:

This Jesus God has raised up, of which we are all witnesses. Therefore being exalted to the right hand of God, and having received from the Father the promise of the Holy Spirit, He poured out this which you now see and hear. (Acts 2:32-33)

Peter concludes:

Repent, and let every one of you be baptized in the name of Jesus Christ for the remission of sins; and you shall receive the gift of the Holy Spirit. (Acts 2:38)

There are further accounts of the outpouring of the Holy Spirit in the Book of Acts. Acts 8 records the experience of Samaritan converts:

Now when the apostles who were at Jerusalem heard that Samaria had received the word of God, they sent Peter and John to them, who, when they had come down, prayed for them that they might receive the Holy Spirit. For as yet He had fallen upon none of them. They had only been baptized in the name of the Lord Jesus. They they laid hands on them, and they received the Holy Spirit. (Acts 8:14-17)

In the case of Saul's dramatic conversion on the road to Damascus there was a three-day delay between his conversion and his being filled with the Holy Spirit. (See Acts 9:1-18.)

Another outpouring of the Holy Spirit occurred at the house of the soldier Cornelius:

While Peter was still speaking these words, the Holy Spirit fell upon all those who heard the word. And those of the circumcision who believed were astonished, as many as came with Peter, because the gift of the Holy Spirit had been poured out on the Gentiles also. For they heard them speak with tongues and magnify God. (Acts 10:44-46)

The final record of a similar outpouring of the Holy Spirit is found in Acts 19:1-6:

And it happened, while Apollos was at Corinth, that Paul, having passed through the upper regions, came to Ephesus. And finding some disciples, he said to them, "Did you receive the Holy Spirit when you believed?" And they said to him, "We have not so much as heard whether there is a Holy Spirit." And he said to them, "Into what then were you baptized?" So they said, "Into John's baptism." Then Paul said, "John indeed baptized with a water of repentance, saying to the people that they should believe on Him who would come after him, that is, on Christ Jesus." When they heard this, they were baptized in the name of the Lord Jesus. And when Paul had laid hands on them, the Holy Spirit came upon them, and they spoke with tongues and prophesied.

These textual records of the outpouring of the Holy Spirit in the Book of Acts form the foundation for the Neo-Pentecostal doctrine of the baptism of the Holy

Spirit. A pattern emerges from the historical narrative that indicates the following:

1. *People were believers and thus born of the Spirit prior to their baptism of the Holy Spirit. This indicates that there must be a distinction between the Spirit's work of regeneration and the Spirit's work in baptizing.*

2. *There is a time gap between faith (regeneration) and Holy Spirit baptism. This clearly indicates that while some Christians have the Holy Spirit to the degree that they are regenerate, they may still lack the baptism of the Holy Spirit, which is subsequent.*

3. *The initial outward evidence of baptism in the Holy Spirit is speaking in tongues.*

When we consider the current debate about the baptism of the Holy Spirit between advocates of Neo-Pentecostal theology and advocates of traditional theology, we see that there is no significant argument concerning Point 1. Virtually all Christian denominations have agreed that there is a difference between the Holy Spirit's work in regeneration (though all do not agree fully on the understanding of regeneration) and the Holy Spirit's work of baptism. That is, though difference abides in the understanding of regeneration and the baptism of the Holy Spirit, there is agreement that whatever each entails, each is different from the other.

It is the second and third conclusions from Acts that spark the debate. Both sides agree that in Acts baptism in the Holy Spirit was indeed subsequent to conversion (at least with some people) and that speaking in tongues was an outward sign or evidence of the Spirit's baptism.

The issue is this: Is the record of Acts proof that the sequence of the Holy Spirit's work among the first Christians is intended to be normative for the church throughout the ages?

The working assumption of Neo-Pentecostal theology is that the purpose of the biblical narrative is to teach us that what happened then was to be normative for all generations. To question this assumption seems, at first glance, to question the authority of Scripture itself. The issue is not the authority of Scripture but the question of the intent of Scripture. It is a question of *interpretation*.

The practical issue that burns within the church is this: Are there two levels of Christians—one kind that has the baptism of the Holy Spirit and another that does not?

This question is further complicated by the record of church history. Though some have bent over backwards trying to prove that there has been a steady stream of speaking in tongues and other evidence of a subsequent Spirit baptism throughout church history, the overwhelming testimony of church history is to the discontinuity of speaking in tongues as an evidence of Spirit baptism.

Church history seems to indicate that the lives of the greatest saints—Athanasius, Augustine, Anselm, Thomas Aquinas, Martin Luther, John Calvin, Jonathan Edwards, Charles H. Spurgeon, and others—failed to display any speaking in tongues indication of having ever been baptized in or by the Holy Spirit.[2] Though speaking in tongues has occurred here and there in church history, it was often associated with heretical movements, such as Montanism in the second century and the Irvingite movement in the nineteenth century.

If speaking in tongues is the outward evidence of Holy Spirit baptism, and the baptism of the Holy Spirit is a crucial and normative subsequent work in the lives of believers, then why have the vast majority of believers in church history failed to attain this vital dimension of Christian life? Was the original Pentecost actually a "failure" for the vast ages of Christian history until the present day? (If the purpose of Pentecost was to pour out a continuous gift of tongues, then the historical discontinuity indicates that the objective was not attained.)

Some have answered this question by posing an eschatological explanation. The first-century phenomenon indicated the "Former Rains" of the Holy Spirit, while the present outpouring or revival of Pentecost indicates the "Latter Rain" of the Holy Spirit and the approaching hour of Christ's return. (The "rains" imagery comes from a prophecy in Joel 2:23.)

This theory would certainly explain the problem of historical discontinuity. However, it would also annul

2. The issue of speaking in tongues was certainly not ignored by the great saints. Luther and Calvin spoke favorably of the gift, though they seem to have connected it with missionary preaching. Wesley also spoke favorably of it. But there is no evidence that these dynamic men of faith ever themselves practiced speaking in tongues.

the theory that the intent of the record in Acts was to convey a normative Christian experience for all ages.

A weaker explanation for historical discontinuity would be the claim that the believers of the past were simply not earnest enough in their pursuit of spirituality to acquire the fullness of the Holy Spirit. This is a possibility, but it hardly seems likely in light of the deep spiritual ardor of some of the saints of the past. There were, and are, devout believers whose lives appear to be models of God-centeredness, yet many (perhaps most) did not speak in tongues.

Again, the heart of the issue comes back to the Neo-Pentecostal assumption that the narrative passages of Acts were intended to teach the church that there will always be a normal time gap between conversion and Spirit baptism and that speaking in tongues is the normal outward sign of Spirit baptism.

I use the word *assumption* here intentionally. Nowhere does the Scripture explicitly teach that speaking in tongues is a necessary sign of the baptism of the Holy Spirit or that there must be a time gap between conversion and Spirit baptism. These ideas are inferences drawn from the narrative. Such inferences may or may not be valid.

I am persuaded that these inferences are not valid. My concern is that these inferences jeopardize the full meaning of Pentecost in church history. My complaint against Neo-Pentecostal theology is that it tends to have too *low* a view of Pentecost. It seems that Neo-Pentecostal theology fails to do justice to the historical significance of the Book of Acts and leaves us with a view of the Spirit's work of charismatic endowment that is more similar to the Old Testament than to the New Testament.

THE HOLY SPIRIT GIFTS
IN THE OLD TESTAMENT

The Holy Spirit was active in the work of redemption in the Old Testament. Regeneration was as much a prerequisite for faith then as it is now. Jesus rebuked Nicodemus, a teacher of Israel, for not understanding that rebirth by the Holy Spirit was necessary for salvation.

In addition to the work of regeneration in quickening the Old Testament believers to faith, the Holy Spirit also dispensed special gifts, or charismatic power, to specific persons. The first people the Scripture mentions to be filled with the Holy Spirit were the craftsmen Bezaleel and Aholiab. They were endowed by the Holy Ghost with power to perform skilled works of art:

And Moses said to the children of Israel, "See, the LORD has called by name Bezaleel the son of Uri, the son of Hur, of the tribe of Judah; and He has filled him with the Spirit of God, in wisdom and understanding, in knowledge and all manner of workmanship, to design artistic works, to work in gold and silver and bronze, in cutting jewels for setting, in carving wood, and to work in all manner of artistic workmanship. And He has put in his heart the ability to teach, in him and Aholiab the son of Ahisamach, of the tribe of Dan." (Exodus 35:30-34)

If we look closely at this narrative we are forced to conclude that Bezaleel and Aholiab were two of the most gifted and versatile artists in human history. They were silversmiths, goldsmiths, jewelers, stone-cutters, and woodcarvers, and they had the gift of teaching as well.

In the Old Testament certain individuals were specially empowered for ministry by the anointing of the Holy Spirit. The prophets spoke under the inspiration of the Spirit. Judges such as Samson, Othniel, and Samuel exhibited special anointings of the Spirit. Even kings were anointed by the Spirit. When David repented of his sin with Bathsheba, he cried out, "Do not take Your Holy Spirit from me" (Psalm 51:11).

It is important to remember that the word *Messiah* has its origin in the Hebrew word for "anointed One." Jesus fulfilled the role of the Old Testament promised Messiah. He was anointed for the messianic task at His baptism:

Then Jesus, when He had been baptized, came up immediately from the water; and behold, the heavens were opened to Him, and He saw the Spirit of God descending like a dove and alighting upon Him. (Matthew 3:16)

Later, at Nazareth, Jesus called attention to the prophecy of Isaiah and declared that it was fulfilled in His own person:

The Spirit of the LORD is upon Me, because He has anointed Me to preach the gospel to the poor. (Luke 4:18)

Perhaps the most dramatic anointing of an individual in the Old Testament was that of Moses. Moses was the mediator of the Old Testament and God's chosen vessel to deliver the Law to Israel. He exercised his leadership over Israel by virtue of the Spirit's charismatic power. A crucial episode for understanding Pentecost takes place in the life of Moses and is recorded in Numbers 11. When the children of Israel complained about their diet of manna, Moses voiced a protest to God: "I am not able to bear all these people alone, because the burden is too heavy for me" (Numbers 11:14).

In response to Moses' burden, God said:

Gather to Me seventy men of the elders of Israel. . . . Then I will come down and talk with you there. I will take of the Spirit that is upon you and will put the same upon them; and they shall bear the burden of the people with you, that you may not bear it yourself alone. (Numbers 11:16-17)

Here we see an expanding distribution of the Holy Spirit. Instead of the Spirit's charismatic power being limited to a solitary isolated individual, God distributes the Holy Spirit to seventy others.

When God accomplished the expanded distribution and the recipients were seen manifesting that power (Numbers 11:20-27), Joshua protested at this apparent encroachment of Moses' power and authority. He said, "Moses my lord, forbid them!" (Numbers 11:28).

Then Moses said to him, "Are you jealous for my sake? Oh, that all the LORD's people were prophets and that the LORD would put His Spirit upon them!" (Numbers 11:29)

Moses' passionate entreaty that God would put His Spirit upon all the Lord's people instead of merely upon some of them became a prophecy in Joel:

148

And it shall come to pass afterward that I will pour out My Spirit on all flesh. (Joel 2:28)

This is the prophecy Peter quotes on the Day of Pentecost. In light of the Old Testament principle of limited distribution of the Holy Spirit, the Day of Pentecost points to the outpouring of the Holy Spirit not on some of God's people but on *all* of God's people.

The difference between the mediator of the Old Covenant—Moses—and the Mediator of the New Covenant—Jesus—is that Jesus distributes His Holy Spirit upon all of His people. This is a key point that is obscured by the Neo-Pentecostal theology. Neo-Pentecostalism grants that the distribution of the Holy Spirit is available for all of God's people but not necessarily gained by all of God's people.

Here is where another interpretation of the Book of Acts is relevant. Before we look again at the pivotal passages in Acts, it may be helpful to engage in a bit of source analysis.

The New Testament science of source criticism involves a technical analysis of various books in an effort to reconstruct the source material that was used to compile the original manuscripts. This is not done for idle academic speculative purposes. One of the crucial rewards of such analysis is the pinpointing of major themes and major concerns of the individual authors of New Testament books.

If we can identify the authors' chief purposes as well as their intended audiences, this goes a long way in helping us understand their teaching with greater accuracy.

For example, when scholars analyze the Synoptic Gospels—Matthew, Mark, and Luke—they are able to isolate material that is unique to each writer. Many scholars believe that Mark was written first and that Matthew and Luke had Mark's Gospel in front of them when they wrote. There is much material in Mark that is duplicated in both Matthew and Luke.

At the same time, there is much material that is common to Matthew and Luke that is not found in Mark. It is apparent that Luke and Matthew used a source that was not available to or not used by Mark. This source is usually called the "Q" source. (The letter *Q* stands for *Quelle*, the German word for "source.")

What concerns us is the material found only in Luke. We call that "L." "L" refers to information that is supplied by Luke that is not found in the other Gospels. By isolating this material we gain insight into Luke's special interests and concerns. (In the case of Matthew the material unique to Matthew—usually called "M"—reveals a strong concern to speak to a Jewish audience).

An examination of Luke indicates that Luke was writing for a Gentile audience and that one of his chief concerns was to show the universality of the gospel.

We know from Scripture that one of the most—possibly *the* most—intense controversies that plagued the early church was the issue of the Gentiles' status in the church. The church began primarily with Jewish believers and then, as Acts relates, spread to the Gentile world, in large part due to Paul's missionary journeys.

It is important to keep in mind that Luke was the author of the Book of Acts. He was intimately aware of the crucial debate about the Gentiles' role in the church.

The Book of Acts follows structurally the mandate of Christ's Great Commission:

But you shall receive power when the Holy Spirit has come upon you; and you shall be witnesses to Me in Jerusalem, and in all Judea and Samaria, and to the end of the earth. (Acts 1:8)

The chronology of Acts follows this pattern of Christianity's spread: Jerusalem—Judea—Samaria—the Gentile world. The narrative begins with events in Jerusalem and then expands outward in the missionary enterprise.

The Day of Pentecost was a Jewish event. It took place in Jerusalem. Pentecost itself was a Jewish feast. The participants were "Jews, devout men, from every nation under heaven" (Acts 2:5). The Jews had come up to Jerusalem for the Feast of Pentecost.

On this occurrence it is important to notice that "they were all filled with the Holy Ghost" (Acts 2:4). There is no evidence here of some believing Jews failing to receive the Holy Spirit. There is no evidence that some earnestly sought the gift while others failed to achieve it. All the Jewish believers experienced the Pentecostal outpouring.

The same phenomenon is seen in the other outpourings recorded in Acts. There is no record in Acts of any believer in a group of believers failing to receive (or only partly receiving) the promised Holy Spirit when He descended. The Spirit comes inclusively and unconditionally.

THE FOUR "PENTECOSTS"

In the early church the question of full inclusion in the body of Christ was not limited merely to the two broad generic groups of Jews and Gentiles. There were *four* distinct groups of people whose status in the church was at issue. These four groups included Jews, Samaritans, God-fearers, and Gentiles. The God-fearers were Gentile converts to Judaism who had embraced the tenets of Judaism but had stopped short of full conversion by opting to remain uncircumcised. It is clear from Acts 10 that Cornelius was a God-fearer.

There was a certain man in Caesarea called Cornelius, a centurion of what was called the Italian Regiment, a devout man and one who feared God with all his household, who gave alms generously to the people, and prayed to God always. (Acts 10:1-2)

It is startling that the four Pentecostal type outpourings recorded in Acts covered precisely the four groups whose status in the church was in question. The Jews received the Holy Spirit at Pentecost. The Samaritans received the Spirit during the ministry of Philip, Peter, and John (Acts 8). The God-fearers received the Holy Spirit at Cornelius's household (Acts 10). And finally there is an outpouring to strictly Gentiles at

Ephesus (Acts 19). All four groups, and all in the groups, received the outpouring of the Holy Spirit.

The question remains: What is the significance of these events? Neo-Pentecostalism finds the significance in the time delay between conversion and receiving the Spirit and in the outward manifestations of tongues.

But that is not the significance of these events stressed by Luke. It is not the chief message the apostles themselves gained from these events.

How did the apostles interpret these events? The key here is found in Acts 10:

While Peter was still speaking these words, the Holy Spirit fell upon all those who heard the word. And those of the circumcision who believed were astonished, as many as came with Peter, because the gift of the Holy Spirit had been poured out on the Gentiles also. For they heard them speak with tongues and magnify God. Then Peter answered, "Can anyone forbid water, that these should not be baptized who have received the Holy Spirit just as we have?" And he commanded them to be baptized in the name of the Lord. (vv. 44-48)

The text indicates that the Jewish believers were shocked to see Gentiles receive the Spirit. The clear meaning of this for Peter was that these converts were to receive full membership in the church. "Can anyone forbid water?" Peter asked. Then he commanded them to be baptized. Here Luke's grand theme of the all-inclusiveness of the New Testament church shines through. There was to be no second-class citizen in the kingdom of God. Jews, Samaritans, God-fearers, and Gentiles all received the baptism of the Holy Spirit.

What is normative about Pentecost is that the Spirit baptizes all the people of God. That there was a time delay in Acts between conversion and baptism does not establish this aspect as a norm. There were clear redemptive-historical reasons for these distinctive "Pentecosts" to occur. They demonstrated clearly the equality of all four groups in the church. There is nothing in the text that indicates such a subsequent time delay to be normative. In Acts 19 Paul asked the Ephesians, "Did you receive the Holy Spirit when you believed?" (Acts 19:2).

By asking this question, Paul apparently held out the possibility that the Ephesians could have received the Pentecostal experience at the time of their conversion, indicating that at least at this point Paul had no concept of a normative time delay. He allowed for the possibility of a time delay but not for the necessity of it.

What about tongues as a necessary evidence for the baptism of the Holy Spirit?

It is clear from the texts of Acts that the gift of speaking tongues did indeed function as an outward sign of the filling of the Spirit. Tongues provided a tangible indication that the Spirit had fallen upon the individual just as the outbreak of ecstatic utterance signaled the reception of the Holy Spirit by Eldad and Medad in Numbers 11. In the case of Jesus, however, in his anointing there was the outward sight of the Spirit descending like a dove

154

(Matthew3:16).[3] At Pentecost there was a visible as well as auditory sign, namely the sight of tongues of fire that sat upon each of them who were filled.

Though these visible signs occurred here and there, it is clear that they were not regarded as necessary or normative indicators of the filling of the Spirit. Though speaking in tongues continued in the life of the church as witnessed by Paul's discussion of the matter in 1 Corinthians, it is clear that by the time 1 Corinthians was written speaking in tongues was not regarded as an indispensable sign of charismatic endowment.

In 1 Corinthians, Paul labors the point that though tongues are a gift from God and therefore profitable, they are not to receive too exalted a status in the church. Paul states his preference this way:

I thank my God I speak with tongues more than you all; yet in the church I would rather speak five words with my understanding, that I may teach others also, than ten thousand words in a tongue. (1 Corinthians 14:18-19)

The apostolic ratio here is 5:10,000. Paul raises a question elsewhere: "Do all speak with tongues?" (1 Corinthians 12:30b). No answer is explicitly given here. However, there is no doubt about that answer. Paul's

3. The account of Jesus' baptism is the basis for using the dove as a symbol of the Holy Spirit. The dove, which has also become a symbol of peace (based on the dove in the Noah's ark account), is not a bad symbol for the Spirit, but it surely does not convey the concept of *power* very well. The rushing wind is a much better symbol, and certainly wind and Spirit have many biblical connections. Fire, as the Pentecost narrative shows, is also an appropriate symbol, but, like both wind and dove, it does not convey the idea of *personality*. It is unfortunate that, on the visual level, there are no really appropriate symbols for the Spirit.

question does not leave its answer open-ended. There can be only one answer to this type of structured question. The answer is no.

In the Corinthian church the gifts of the Spirit were highly evident and operative. Yet Paul again labors the point that the Spirit gifts His people with a diversity of gifts.

Now there are diversities of gifts, but the same Spirit. There are differences of ministries, but the same Lord. And there are diversities of activities, but it is the same God who works all in all. But the manifestation of the Spirit is given to each one for the profit of all: for to one is given the word of wisdom through the Spirit, to another the word of knowledge through the same Spirit, to another faith. . . . But one and the same Spirit works all these things, distributing to each one individually as He wills. (1 Corinthians 12:4-11)

The Holy Spirit sovereignly gifts His church. The church is a body of gifted members who function within the framework of unity and diversity. No office or gift is to be elevated to the level of an exclusive sign of the Spirit's manifestation.

Paul further states:

For by one Spirit we were all baptized into one body— whether Jews or Greeks, whether slaves or free—and have all been made to drink into one Spirit. (1 Corinthians 12:13)

Dale Bruner comments on this passage:

If this verse is interpreted as speaking of a second, subsequent and separate baptism in the Holy Spirit, beyond bap-

*tism in Christ, for only some Christians, then violence is
done not only to the words of the text—"all . . . all"—but
to the purpose of the text in its Corinthian context. . . . In
1 Corinthians 12:13 Paul is not teaching a universal baptism won by only a few, he is teaching the gracious Christian baptism through the Spirit given to all.*[4]

The weight of the biblical interpretation of the meaning of Pentecost militates against the Neo-Pentecostal
understanding of the baptism of the Holy Spirit. All
whom the Spirit regenerates He also baptizes, fills, and
endows with power for ministry.

This is the exciting news of Pentecost. In God's plan
of redemption the Holy Spirit has gifted every believer
for ministry. The whole church has been empowered
from on high. There are not two levels of believers—
gifted and nongifted, baptized in the Spirit and not
baptized in the Spirit.[5]

We hear abundant testimony from modern Christians
who declare that their experience of baptism in the
Spirit and speaking in tongues has dramatically changed
their spiritual lives. They have more zeal, more bold-
ness, more earnestness in prayer. It has been said that a
man with an experience is never at the mercy of a man
with an argument.

I have no quarrel with people's experiences with the

4. Frederick Dale Bruner, *A Theology of the Holy Spirit* (Grand Rapids:
Eerdmans, 1970), 292.

5. Many Charismatics and Pentecostals emphasize other gifts of the
Spirit—healing, prophesying, leadership, hospitality, discernment, exhor-
tation, interpretation, etc. It is unfortunate that, in the minds of many
Christians, speaking in tongues has come to be seen as *the* evidence of
Spirit baptism.

Holy Spirit. I am delighted to hear of increased faith, zeal, earnestness in prayer, and the rest. My concern is not with the meaningfulness of the experience but with the understanding of the meaning of the experience. It is the interpretation of the experience that tends to go against Scripture. Our authority is not our experience but the Word of God. People in the church do not all have the same experience in the Spirit, but this does not indicate that they do not all have the same Spirit. This is the very issue that so deeply troubled the Corinthian church.

I am not saying that everyone who is a member of a Christian church has the Holy Spirit. Membership in the visible church no more guarantees the baptism of the Holy Spirit than it guarantees salvation. We know that there are unbelievers who are church members. No unbeliever has the baptism of the Holy Spirit, but every believer, every regenerate person, does have the baptism of the Holy Spirit. Every Christian from Pentecost to the present is both regenerate of the Spirit and baptized in the Spirit. That is the essence of the meaning of Pentecost. Anything less casts a shadow over the sacred importance of Pentecost in the history of redemption. Any person who is regenerate is also sealed by the Spirit, baptized in the Spirit, and has the earnest of the Spirit.

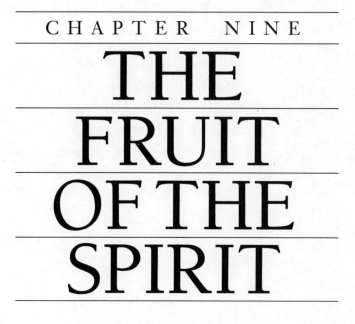

CHAPTER NINE

THE FRUIT OF THE SPIRIT

God sealed you by giving you
the gift of his Holy Spirit.
Every child of God bears the same seal,
is indwelt by the same Holy Spirit.

TOM REES

THE GIFTS of the Holy Spirit are fascinating and exciting. To be a gifted person is to receive accolades from our fellows for our performances or abilities. For these reasons and perhaps others, the gifts of the Spirit receive far more attention in our culture than the fruit of the Spirit. The fruits of the Spirit seem to be doomed to obscurity, hidden in the shadow of the more preferred gifts.

Yet it is the evidence of the fruit of the Spirit that is the mark of our progress in sanctification. Of course, God is pleased when we dutifully exercise the gifts the Holy Spirit has bestowed upon us. But I think God is even more pleased when He sees His people manifest the fruit of the Spirit.

Paul exhorts the Galatians:

I say then: Walk in the Spirit, and you shall not fulfill the lust of the flesh. (Galatians 5:16)

The Christian life is a pilgrimage. In the imagery of the Scripture, it is a journey that we travel by foot. Walking is a relatively slow mode of transportation. Most of us move along this journey at a snail's pace. We do not race and leap through the obstacle course of temptation. There are barriers that impede our progress. At every point we face the speed-bumps of the flesh. Again Paul writes:

For the flesh lusts against the Spirit, and the Spirit against the flesh; and these are contrary to one another, so that you do not do the things that you wish. (Galatians 5:17)

Here is the battle. The old man is pitted against the new man. The sin nature of the flesh fights to choke the influence of the Spirit. Though this warfare is internal and invisible, there are clear outward signs of the carnage wrought by the battle. When the Spirit is victorious, we see the fruit of it. When the flesh wins, we also see the outward evidence.

Before Paul elaborates the fruit of the Spirit, he first sets forth the works of the flesh. The works of the flesh stand in stark contrast to the fruit of the Spirit.

Now the works of the flesh are evident, which are: adultery, fornication, uncleanness, licentiousness, idolatry, sorcery, hatred, contentions, jealousies, outbursts of wrath, selfish ambitions, dissensions, heresies, envy, murders, drunkenness, revelries, and the like; of which I tell you beforehand, just as I also told you in time past, that those who practice such things will not inherit the kingdom of God. (Galatians 5:19-21)

This list of the works of the flesh is crucial for two reasons. First, it offers the contrast already mentioned to the fruit of the Spirit. Second, it identifies sinful practices that, the Apostle emphasizes (by repetition), characterize the unregenerate and the lost. Of course, it is possible for a redeemed person to fall into any of these sins for a season. Each one of them has been manifested at one time or another by the greatest of saints. But they are not to be characteristic of the Christian. If this list characterizes the life-style of a person, it is evidence that he is unredeemed.

Because this list carries such an ominous warning, it is important to give brief definition to the sins mentioned:

1. Adultery. *The first sin mentioned is a prohibition of the Seventh Commandment. It involves the violation of the sanctity of marriage via illicit sexual relations among married persons.*

2. Fornication. *Fornication usually has reference to sexual intercourse among unmarried people. It is usually associated with premarital sexual intercourse. In this text, however, it has a broader meaning to include illegitimate sexual intercourse in the widest sense of the word. (Homosexual acts are included under this.)*

3. Uncleanness. *There is a sexual sense implied here. It reflects a kind of behavior that popular language calls "dirty."*

4. Licentiousness. *This describes a wild, unruly life-style that is unrestrained and out of control.*

5. Idolatry. *This refers to the pagan worship of idols or false gods. Idolatry in its broadest sense can include such things as worship of material possessions.*

6. Sorcery. *This involves the practice of magic and the involvement with forbidden practices such as spiritualism, fortune-telling, astrology, and the like.*

7. Hatred. *This reflects a character of hostility, grudge-bearing, and being unloving.*

8. Contentions. *This is seen in a quarrelsome attitude. One who is contentious is argumentative and combative. He has a chip on his shoulder.*

9. Jealousies. *Jealousy reflects a self-centered spirit that despises other people's achievements or victories. It displays a lack of love. Works 7, 8, and 9 are probably some of the pet sins of Christians, possibly because they can be so easily concealed or explained away.*

10. Outbursts of wrath. *This indicates a character of hot-headed temper fits.*

11. Selfish ambitions. *This contains the idea of a ruthless desire for personal gain at the expense of others.*

12. Dissensions. *This does not rule out legitimate forms of dissent. Rather, it characterizes again the contentious spirit that is constantly bickering, feuding, and creating dissension in groups.*

13. Heresies. *The root meaning of this involves a willful choosing of opinions that go against established truth. It includes more than theological errors, for it can also refer to attitudinal and behavioral errors.*

14. Envy. *Envy involves the desire to possess what belongs to someone else. This can include nurturing ill will toward those who enjoy certain benefits.*

15. Murders. *This is self-explanatory. Most Christians are not outright murderers, of course, but Christ's words about hating one's brother (Matthew 5:22) should be kept in mind.*

16. Drunkenness. *This refers to the intemperate use of alcohol and, by implication, drug abuse.*

17. Revelries. *This involves the life-style of the wild party goer who enjoys uninhibited orgies or drinking bouts.*

Over against this list of the works of the flesh Paul sets forth the fruit of the Spirit:

The fruit of the Spirit is love, joy, peace, longsuffering, kindness, goodness, faithfulness, gentleness, self-control. Against such there is no law. (Galatians 5:22-23)

Here the Apostle exhibits the model of authentic righteousness. The fruit is designated as the fruit of the Spirit. Fruit is something that is produced in us. It is not of ourselves. In ourselves we are only flesh. The flesh produces nothing but more flesh. The deeds of the flesh are the fruit of the flesh. The flesh profits nothing. Martin Luther declared that "nothing" is not a "little something."

Like begets like. The product comes from the producer. The progeny recapitulates the ontogeny. Only the Holy Spirit can conceive and bear the fruit of the Spirit. We can be skilled preachers without the Spirit. We can be theological geniuses after the flesh. We can be silver-tongued orators apart from grace. But the only source of the fruit of the Spirit is the work of the Holy Spirit within us.

It is no accident that the fruit of the Spirit is not elevated in our ranks as the highest test of righteousness. There abides so much flesh in us that we prefer another standard. The fruit test is too high; we cannot attain it. So within our Christian subcultures we prefer to elevate some lesser test by which we can measure ourselves with more success. We can compete with each other with greater facility if we mix some flesh together with Spirit.

How hard it is for us to be measured by our love! And please don't evaluate me by the standard of gentleness. I'm far too impatient to deserve patience as my standard of growth. It is easier for me to preach than to forbear. It is easier for me to write a book about peace than to practice peace.

The fruit of the Spirit includes a list of virtues that on the surface appear to be commonplace. John Calvin spoke of virtues that unregenerate pagans are capable of displaying to some degree. He described the "civil righteousness" achieved by natural man. By the common grace of God, fallen creatures exhibit an external form of righteousness.

External righteousness is that which outwardly corresponds to the law of God but lacks the motivation from a heart disposed toward the love of God. Unbelievers can love by a natural affection. Unbelieving husbands have a natural affection for their wives. Unbelieving mothers have a natural affection for their children. Secular music extols the virtue of love.

So also the other virtues mentioned as the fruit of the Spirit may be manifest among the ungodly. There were moments when Adolph Hitler was kind. Stalin had momentary displays of gentleness. The Pharaoh of Moses' Egypt at times lapsed into patience. In our own day the Mormons are noted for being temperate.

Herein is the problem. If unbelievers can exhibit the virtues mentioned in the fruit of the Spirit, how can we know if the presence of these virtues in any way indicates the presence of the Spirit in our lives? Not a single fruit of the Spirit, externally exhibited, is a proof of regeneration.

Perhaps it is because of the facility of confusion

between "civil righteousness" and the fruit of the Spirit that Christians tend to look elsewhere for indicators of true godliness. But the Bible would not have us yield to this temptation. The Spirit yields authentic fruit. It is His work that we are to cultivate in our lives. (Since even unbelievers can be kind, gentle, peaceful, etc., Christians often focus on such concerns as eloquent preaching, writing, etc. Being good—showing the fruit of the Spirit—in an unobtrusive way is less dramatic but possibly more godly than being an excellent preacher, religious author, gospel singer, etc.)

We must learn to discern the difference between civil righteousness and the fruit of the Spirit. The difference is more than one of degree. It is a difference of kind as well.

The fruit of the Spirit is uncommon and extraordinary. It is the difference, for example, between a love that is common and a love that is uncommon, between ordinary love and extraordinary love, between natural love and supernatural love.

LOVE

The fruit of love that is born of the Holy Spirit is a transcendent love. It rises above the commonplace virtue of natural affection. It is the biblical *agape*, the love that is rhapsodized in 1 Corinthians 13. It is one thing to love the lovely. It is quite another to love one's enemies. Natural love is like gold mixed with an abundance of dross. It is tarnished by selfish interests. It is mixed with the lead of envy and the alloy of rudeness. It is an inconsistent love.

Paul, in 1 Corinthians 13, tells us that love does not envy, boast, or exhibit pride. It is not rude, self-seeking, or easily angered. It keeps no records of wrongs received. It does not delight in evil.

Love is not defined by simplistic abstinence from drinking, dancing, makeup, movies, card-playing, and the like. It was envy that required the cross, not lipstick; it was covetousness that demanded atonement, not poker; it was pride that called forth the need for propitiation, not the cinema.

Some describe true love as "unconditional love." This concept can be either a coin of pure gold or a gilded rock in the fraud's bag of tricks. It is at once true or grossly false depending upon how it is understood. The preacher who smiles benignly from his pulpit, assuring us that "God accepts you just the way you are" tells a monstrous lie. The kingdom of God is far more rigorous in its requirements than Mr. Rogers's neighborhood. The gospel of love may not be sugarcoated with saccharin grace. God does not accept the arrogant man in his arrogance. He turns His holy back on the impenitent. To be sure, He demonstrates love toward His fallen creatures, but that love has holy demands. We must come to Him on bended knee and with a contrite heart.

Jonathan Edwards spoke of love in this way:

If love is the sum of Christianity, surely those things which overthrow love are exceedingly unbecoming to Christians. An envious Christian, a malicious Christian, a cold and hard-hearted Christian, is the greatest absurdity and con-tradiction. It is as if one should speak of dark brightness, or a false truth.

My teacher Dr. John Gerstner once spoke of the manifestation of *agape* in the life of the apostle Paul. He used the four letters of Paul's name as an acrostic to describe the man's character. The *P* stood for *P*olluted, since Paul described himself as the chief of sinners. The *A* stood for his *A*postolic office. But it is the *U* and the *L* that are relevant here. The *U* referred to Paul's *U*ncompromising commitment to truth, the *L* for Paul's quality of *L*ove. Gerstner put it this way: "It is not that we say Paul was uncompromising *and* loving. Or even that he was uncompromising *but* loving. Rather, we say that Paul was uncompromising, *therefore* loving."

Spiritual love is wrought by God. We are able to love Him because He first loved us and because it is His love that is shed abroad in our hearts. This love transcends natural affection. It flows from a heart that has been changed by God the Holy Spirit.

JOY

Joy is mentioned as a fruit of the Spirit. This joy is not the joy we encounter for a moment when our favorite team wins the Super Bowl. It is not that "happiness of a warm puppy." Like transcendent *agape* love, the Christian's joy is a transcendent joy, a joy born of blessedness. An unbeliever experiences positive emotions that evoke smiles, but no unbeliever has ever experienced the beatific joy of salvation.

The joy of the Spirit is permanent. This year's Super Bowl winner may not make the playoffs next season. Warm puppies grow cold in the grave. The joy of salvation is forever. The victory Christ has won for us is not seasonal. The Savior never has a bad year.

The joy of the Spirit is as stable as it is exhilarating. It is the joy that abides in the midst of suffering. It has depth. It penetrates the soul. It sends despair into exile and banishes pessimism. It produces confidence without arrogance, courage without bravado. Jesus of Nazareth was able to weep. Yet His tears could not dissolve the joy He knew in His Father's house.

We rejoice in our hope. Our hope is not the fantasy of the dreamer but the assurance of the redeemed. It is the joy of those who have ears to hear the Savior's command, "Be of good cheer, for I have overcome the world" (John 16:33).

PEACE

The peace of the Spirit is likewise transcendent. It is the peace, the *shalom* for which every Jew yearned. It goes beyond what Martin Luther called a carnal peace, the peace offered by the false prophets of Israel. It is not the cowardly peace won by appeasement. It is a peace wrought by permanent victory.

When earthly wars are ended and the peace treaties are signed, there always abides an uneasy truce. A cold war always remains, wherein the slightest rattle of the sword may signal the beginning of new hostilities. There is a vast difference between Neville Chamberlain's leaning over a balcony declaring, "We have achieved peace in our time" and Jesus' leaning over a table to say, "Peace I leave with you, My peace I give unto you; not as the world gives do I give to you" (John 14:27).

The legacy of Christ is peace. Peace is our inheritance from the Prince of Peace. It is a peace the world cannot give. This peace is a lasting peace that no one can snatch from us.

The Holy Spirit gives us an inner peace, a peace that passes understanding. But the peace He gives is infinitely more valuable than peace of mind. It transcends the imperturbability of the Stoic and the *ataraxia* of the Epicurean. It is the peace that flows from our justification. Being justified, we have peace with God. We have heard and received the gospel. We have heard the clarion call of God. "Comfort, yes, comfort My people! . . . Speak comfort to Jerusalem, and cry out to her, that her warfare is ended, that her iniquity is pardoned" (Isaiah 40:1-2).

The worst holocaust of history is the war between a holy God and His rebellious creatures. For the Christian that war is over, once and for all. We may continue to sin and incur God's displeasure. We may grieve the Spirit, but He will never again declare war upon us. It was ratified for us on the cross.

LONG-SUFFERING (PATIENCE)
The fruit of the Spirit is long-suffering—that is, patience. This virtue mirrors and reflects the character of God. It

has no place for explosive tantrums from a hair-trigger personality. It is slow to anger. It endures the insult and the malice of others. It knows nothing of a judgmental spirit.

It is the stuff of which Job was made when he declared, "Though He slay me, yet will I trust Him" (Job 13:15). It has a capacity to wait. Waiting is difficult. We wait for planes and buses. We wait for mail and for visitors. We wait for Christ to return. We wait for the promise of His vindication.

The Christian rejects the spirit of pragmatism. He lives in terms of long-term goals. He eschews the expedient. He stores up treasure in heaven. He is willing to wait for the hour of God.

The Spirit is patient with people. The fruit He gives enables us to forbear with each other. We do not demand the instant sanctification of our brothers. Patience and long-suffering do not rail against the speck in our brother's eye. They are married to the love that covers a multitude of sins.

KINDNESS

Jesus was strong and tender. When He encountered the powerful and arrogant, He asked no quarter and gave none. When He met the weak and brokenhearted, He was tender. He never broke a bruised reed. His rebuke of the sinner was couched in kindness. "Neither do I condemn you; go and sin no more" (John 8:11) was His response to a humiliated woman. The Judge of all the earth was not harsh. He took no glee in condemnation.

Kindness is a virtue of grace. It involves a willingness to keep one's power and authority in check. It does not crush the weak. It is thoughtful and kind. It manifests the judgment of charity, tempering justice with mercy.

GOODNESS

Goodness incorporates a basic personal integrity. The fruit of the Spirit promotes a person of guilelessness. Goodness is a relative term. Something or someone is good relative to some standard. The ultimate standard of goodness is the character of God Himself. This is why Jesus said to the rich young ruler, "Why do you call Me good? No one is good but One, that is, God" (Luke 18:19).

Yet the quality of goodness is planted in the lives wherein the Holy Spirit works. He works goodness within us. Though our best works remain tainted by sin, nevertheless a real change is wrought within us. In salvation we gain a cure as well as a pardon. He is making us well.

Not only does God declare us just by the imputation of Christ's righteousness, He indwells us to make us what He declares us to be. Sanctification follows justification. That sanctification is as real as our justification. The fruit is goodness.

FAITHFULNESS

Faith is a gift of God. It is also a fruit. The faith by which we are saved is not of our own doing. It comes from

God. But it comes *to* us and is exercised by us. The Spirit works faith in us. This is Luther's *fides viva*, the living faith that yields works of obedience.

Faith is trust. It means far more than believing in God. It means believing God. The fruit of the Spirit involves trusting God with our lives.

But the fruit of faith involves more than trust. It means that we become trustworthy. A person of faith is not only a person who trusts but a person who can be trusted. His yea means yea and his nay means nay. He keeps his word. He pays his bills. He meets his obligations. He is faithful. He is loyal. Fidelity is a mark of his character.

GENTLENESS

Gentleness is a godly virtue. A man who is gentle is a gentleman. To be an authentic gentleman is to model Christ. Polls in women's magazines repeatedly reveal that the twin virtues women desire in men are strength and tenderness.

Gentleness—meekness—is not to be confused with weakness. Moses was a meek man. That is, he had the quality of humility. He knew who he was. He was bold without being arrogant. It is the meek who are promised the world. Christ promises they will inherit the earth. Meekness is the flip side of gentleness. They go together, wed by a spirit of humility.

God gives grace to the humble. It is a grace that breeds even more grace.

SELF-CONTROL

The last fruit of the Spirit in the list—self-control, or temperance—flows from the other virtues. Immodesty, extremism, and flamboyance do not fit with temperance. Here the moderate level of self-control is manifested. The Spirit is not rude or pushy. He is neither violent nor crude.

These are the fruits of the Holy Spirit. These are the genuine marks of godliness. These are the virtues we see eminently and vividly modeled in the lives of mature Christians.

These are the virtues our Lord wants us to cultivate. These are the virtues that are at the same time the gifts of God. God promises to reward these traits in us, not because they flow from our own intrinsic righteousness, but because, as Augustine put it, "God is pleased to crown His own gifts."

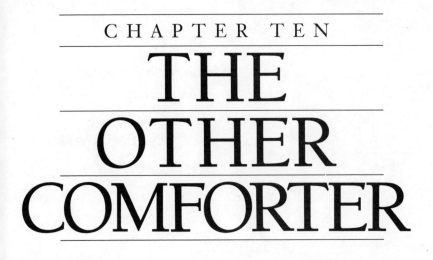

CHAPTER TEN

THE OTHER COMFORTER

*Man may dismiss compassion
from his heart,
but God will never.*

WILLIAM COWPER

ON THE EVE of His death Jesus met with His disciples in the Upper Room. He expressed a deep longing to celebrate the Passover with His friends before He entered into His sufferings. At such a time we might expect Jesus to look to His friends for comfort and support. Instead Jesus is working to comfort *them*.

In the Upper Room Jesus gives His longest recorded discourse on the Person and work of the Holy Spirit. In this discourse Jesus promises that He will send the Holy Spirit:

I will pray the Father, and He will give you another Helper, that He may abide with you forever, even the Spirit of truth, whom the world cannot receive, because it neither sees Him nor knows Him; but you know Him, for He dwells with you and will be in you. I will not leave you orphans; I will come to you. (John 14:16-18)

Here Jesus speaks of "another Helper." The word that is translated "Helper" or "Comforter" or "Counselor" is the Greek word *paraclete*.

The first thing we notice is that Jesus promises "another" Paraclete. This means that the promised Paraclete is clearly not the first to appear on the scene. For if there is to be "another" of anything, there must be at least one prior to it.

I labor this point because it is customary in the language of the church to speak of the Holy Spirit as *the*

Paraclete. Indeed, the title of Paraclete is used almost exclusively for the Holy Spirit.

But we must insist that the Holy Spirit is not *the* Paraclete. *The* Paraclete is Jesus Christ. Jesus' role of Paraclete is vitally important to His early ministry. The Holy Spirit assumes the title of "Another Paraclete" in light of Jesus' absence. The Spirit is sent to be Christ's early "substitute" or "replacement." The Spirit is the Supreme Vicar of Christ on earth.

JESUS AS OUR PARACLETE

To understand Jesus' role as our Paraclete, let us look at the birth narratives in Luke's Gospel. In the record of Jesus' presentation at Jerusalem we read this account:

There was a man in Jerusalem whose name was Simeon, and this man was just and devout, waiting for the Consolation of Israel, and the Holy Spirit was upon him. (Luke 2:25)

In this text the phrase "Consolation of Israel" functions as a term for the coming Messiah. Simeon had been promised that "he would not see death before he had seen the Lord's Christ" (Luke 2:26). (Both words— Christ in Greek and Messiah in Hebrew—mean "anointed one.")

In Old Testament Judaism the concept of the "Consolation of Israel" expresses the hope of messianic salvation. Comforting His people is a work of God. God has the power to transform desolation into consolation. We hear the promise of God in Isaiah:

"Comfort, yes, comfort My people!" says your God. "Speak comfort to Jerusalem, and cry out to her, that her warfare is ended, that her iniquity is pardoned; for she has received from the LORD's hand double for all her sins." (Isaiah 40:1-2)

The image of God's comfort of His people is expressed in the shepherd image:

He will feed His flock like a shepherd; He will gather the lambs with His arm, and carry them in His bosom, and gently lead those who are with young. (Isaiah 40:11)

The consolation of Jerusalem is linked to the image of God as a comforting mother:

Rejoice with Jerusalem, and be glad with her, all you who love her; rejoice for joy with her, all you who mourn for her; that you may feed and be satisfied with the consolation of her bosom. . . . As one whom his mother comforts, so I will comfort you; And you shall be comforted in Jerusalem. (Isaiah 66:10-13)

The greatest comforter sent by God for the consolation of His people is His Suffering Servant. In Isaiah's description of the role of the Servant of God we read:

The Spirit of the Lord God is upon Me, because the LORD has anointed Me to preach good tidings to the poor; He has sent Me to heal the brokenhearted, to proclaim liberty to the captives, and the opening of the prison to those who are bound; to proclaim the acceptable year of the LORD, and the day of vengeance of our God; to comfort all who mourn, to console those who mourn in Zion, to give them beauty for ashes, the oil of joy for mourning, the garment of praise for the spirit of heaviness. (Isaiah 61:1-3)

These words are echoed in part by Jesus in the Sermon on the Mount: "Blessed are those who mourn, for they shall be comforted" (Matthew 5:4).

The ministry of the Messiah involves a ministry of consolation. He comes to heal the brokenhearted and to comfort all who mourn. It is the Messiah, Jesus Himself, who is the Paraclete. It is only in His announced departure from this world that He proclaims the sending of "another" Paraclete.

WHAT IS A PARACLETE?

Though we have sketched out a brief profile of the role of consolation in the ministry of Christ, we turn now from the basic concept of consolation to the title of Paraclete itself.

The term *Paraclete* had a rich and varied usage in the ancient world. The word is derived from a prefix (*para-*) and root (*kalein*) which together mean "one who is called alongside."

In the ancient world a paraclete was someone summoned to give assistance in a court of law. The paraclete was a legal adviser who pleaded a person's case in court. This is the central sense in which it is used in 1 John:

My little children, these things I write to you, that you may not sin. And if anyone sins, we have an Advocate with the Father, Jesus Christ the righteous. (2:1)

Here the word translated "Advocate" is *Paraclete*. There is no doubt in this passage that it is Jesus, not the Holy Spirit, who is called Paraclete.

In this passage the Paraclete is an Advocate before the bar of God. The tremendous truth of the New Testament is that when we stand before the tribunal of God, the presiding judge at our trial will be Jesus. At the same time our court-appointed defense attorney will also be Jesus. It is not a frightening thought to go to trial when one is secure in the knowledge that the judge is also our defense attorney.

We see a graphic display in the role of Jesus as Advocate in the record of the stoning of Stephen:

And they stirred up the people, the elders, and the scribes; and they came upon him, seized him, and brought him to the council. They also set up false witnesses who said, "This man does not cease to speak blasphemous words against this holy place and the law." (Acts 6:12-13)

Stephen underwent the mockery of a trial with trumped-up charges against him. The earthly assembly behaved like a kangaroo court. After Stephen gave a ringing speech as his defense, his judges reacted with unbridled fury:

When they heard these things they were cut to the heart, and they gnashed at him with their teeth. (Acts 7:54)

In their anger and hostility the early tribunal lashed out in judgment against Stephen. In this precise moment, by the grace of God, Stephen was given a remarkable vision into the court of heaven:

But he, being full of the Holy Spirit, gazed into heaven and saw the glory of God, and Jesus standing at the right hand of God, and said, "Look! I see the heavens opened

and the Son of Man standing at the right hand of God!"
(Acts 7:55-56)

Stephen said, "Look!" Surely if he hadn't been beside
himself from ecstasy for the glorious vision he was enjoy-
ing, he would have realized that nothing would be more
futile than to tell his accusers to look. They couldn't
possibly see what God was allowing his eyes to witness.

Beyond his excited charge to look is the crucial importance of what Stephen actually saw. He saw Jesus standing at the right hand of God.

The church has an important doctrine called the
Session (from the Latin *sessio*) of Christ. Christ's session
refers to His exalted position of being seated at the right
hand of God. This session involves Christ's investiture
with cosmic authority. He occupies the seat of preemi-
nent authority. From this seat at the right hand of God,
Jesus exercises kingly dominion and judicial power. He
is both king and judge.

However in the vision of Stephen, Jesus is not seated.
He stands. In a courtroom the judge is seated at the
bench. The only time the judge stands is to enter and
depart the courtroom. During the trial itself, the judge
remains seated. When the case is being tried, the prosecuting attorney stands to interrogate witnesses, or to
address the jury or approach the bench. Likewise the
defense counsel stands when it is his turn to try the case.

The supreme irony of Stephen's vision is that at the
very moment his earthly tribunal is condemning him to
death as a theological heretic, the Prince of Theology

rises in the court of heaven to plead Stephen's case for him before the Father. When Jesus stands, He rises as Stephen's Advocate. He is Stephen's Paraclete in heaven.

What Jesus did for Stephen was not an isolated event. He does the same thing for all who are His people. He is our Advocate, even now.

The role of Jesus as our Advocate before the Father is so important that we dare not let it be obscured in our understanding of the ministry of the Holy Spirit as Paraclete.

The Holy Spirit is our "other" Paraclete, our sacred Advocate. In his role as Paraclete He performs more than one task.

In the first place, the Holy Spirit assists us in addressing the Father:

Likewise the Spirit also helps in our weaknesses. For we do not know what we should pray for as we ought, but the Spirit Himself makes intercession for us with groanings which cannot be uttered. Now He who searches the hearts knows what the mind of the Spirit is, because He makes intercession for the saints according to the will of God. (Romans 8:26-27)

One of the most vital ingredients of prayer is that our prayers should be according to the will of God. Prayer itself is a form of worship. God requires that our worship be in spirit and in truth. Just as we enjoy two Advocates with the Father, so also do we have two Intercessors with the Father. The Holy Spirit assists us in praying properly to the Father.

In secular popular jargon, a lawyer is sometimes referred to as a "mouthpiece." We remember the fear that gripped Moses when God called him to lead the Exodus out of Egypt. Moses was troubled by his feelings of inadequacy as a speaker. He cried out to God:

"O my Lord, I am not eloquent, neither before nor since You have spoken to Your servant; but I am slow of speech and slow of tongue." So the LORD said to him, "Who has made man's mouth? Or who makes the mute, the deaf, the seeing, or the blind? Have not I, the LORD? Now therefore, go, and I will be with your mouth and teach you what you shall say." (Exodus 4:10-12)

When Moses continued to protest, God promised to give him Aaron as his spokesman:

Now you shall speak to him and put the words in his mouth. And I will be with your mouth and with his mouth, and I will teach you what you shall do. So he shall be your spokesman to the people. (Exodus 4:15-16)

Here we see the Maker of man's mouth stooping to aid His lisping children. The Holy Spirit is our Paraclete, not only before the Father but before human beings as well. What God promises Moses in the Old Testament is substantively promised to all of God's children in the New Testament.

Jesus promised His disciples that in their moment of crisis the Holy Spirit would be there to assist them in speaking before men:

But when they arrest you and deliver you up, do not worry beforehand, or premeditate what you shall speak. But what-

ever is given you in that hour, speak that; for it is not you who speak, but the Holy Spirit. (Mark 13:11)

We see then that the Holy Spirit serves as our Advocate or Paraclete before the Father as well as before the tribunals of this world.

At the same time the Spirit works to defend us, He works to convict the world of sin. He is our defense attorney, while at the same time exercising the role of prosecuting attorney against the world:

And when He has come, He will convict the world of sin, and of righteousness, and of judgment: of sin, because they do not believe in Me; of righteousness, because I go to My Father and you see Me no more; of judgment, because the ruler of this world is judged. (John 16:8-11)

We see then that in His role as Paraclete the primary task of the Holy Spirit is forensic or legal. This dimension of His activity is consistent with His nature and character. He is the Spirit of truth and the Spirit of holiness. The Spirit bears witness to the truth of Christ. Unbelief in Jesus is a sin. The world is convicted of the sin of unbelief. In the Spirit's prosecution of the world, He is at the same time working to vindicate us through Christ. The Holy Spirit stands always on the side of truth and righteousness.

THE PARACLETE AND COMFORT

When we see that the primary role of the Paraclete is that of a defense counselor, we wonder how this is linked to the concept of comfort or consolation.

As we have already seen, there is a linguistic link between the term *Consolation of Israel* and the title *Paraclete*. Both the word *consolation* and the title *Paraclete* are derived from the same word forms. (*Consolation* is *paraklesis* in Greek.)

Though it is important to distinguish between the Spirit's work of consolation and His work of intercessory assistance before God and man, we cannot separate them. Part of the consolation we enjoy is the certain knowledge that the Holy Spirit is called alongside of us in our time of trial.

There is another critical distinction, however, that must be kept in mind. When we think of comfort or consolation, we usually think of it in terms of being ministered to after we are wounded. A mother consoles a weeping child. We are given comfort by the Spirit when we are in mourning.

Surely the Holy Spirit does these tender acts of ministry for God's people. The Spirit is the Author of the peace that passes understanding. But in His role of Paraclete the Spirit is doing something to assist us before we are wounded. He works to provide us with strength for the battle as well as consoling us after the battle.

The title *Paraclete* in older versions of the English Bible was normally translated by the English word *Comforter*. Most modern translation we have seen substitute a different English word, such as *Helper* or *Counselor*. This does not reflect an error in the earlier translations. Rather, it calls attention to the changeability of human language. Our common forms of speech tend to undergo transition as popular usage changes.

For example, the word *cute* used to mean "bow-legged." And consider the word *scan.* What would you do if your teacher told you to scan your textbook? Most people would take that directive to mean "leaf lightly through the book." Here is a case where a word is defined almost exactly opposite from its original meaning. Originally *scan* meant "to read with strict precision, paying close attention." When we are riding in an airplane, we hope that those who are scanning the radar screens that are tracking our flights are doing it with more than casual attention. Perhaps the change in the word *scan* is due to its similar sound to the word *skim.* In today's usage scanning means skimming, where originally they were opposite terms.

Something similar has evolved with the understanding of the word *comfort.* We think of comfort almost totally in terms of ministering to our sorrow and grief by way of tender support. The word comes from Latin. It has a prefix (*com-*, meaning "with") and a root (*fortis*, meaning "strong"). So the word originally meant "with strength." Thus a comforter was someone who came to give strength for the battle rather than solace after the battle.

Of course, the Holy Spirit does both. He is the most tender source of solace the wounded, the defeated, or the grief-stricken person can know. But the emphasis on the promised Paraclete is that He will come to give us strength and assistance for the battle.

Sometimes we hear the expression "that is not my forte." When a person says that, he is declaring that he is weak in a certain area. *Forte* is used popularly as a synonym for strength.

In biblical terms it is the Holy Spirit who is our forte. He is the One from whom we derive our strength. It is because the promised Holy Spirit has come and dwells in us and stands with us that the Scriptures can declare:

In all these things we are more than conquerors through Him who loved us. (Romans 8:37)

One of the ironies of history is found in the criticism of Christianity by the German philosopher Frederick Nietzsche. Nietzsche complained that Christianity was a religion of weakness, a religion that caused men to deny their most fundamental drive, the "will to power."

In declaring the death of God, Nietzsche said that God died of pity. Pity, tenderness, and weak-kneed timidity have been the legacy of Christianity to the world. Nietzsche called for a new humanity that would be ushered in by the Superman. The chief character trait of the Superman would be courage. Above all else, the Superman would be a conqueror.

Here is the irony of Romans 8. When Paul says that we are "more than conquerors," it takes us three words to translate a single Greek word. The Greek word is *hupernikon*. The prefix *huper-* comes across into English as our word *hyper.* Literally, Paul writes that Christians are not only conquerors, they are "hyper-conquerors." (The Latin translation of *hupernikon* is *supervincemus.* So the Latin actually reads, "We are *super*-conquerors.")

If Nietzsche is looking for supermen, he must look to those who have been strengthened by the power and presence of God the Holy Spirit, the Spirit who is called alongside of us to come with strength.

Indeed, in and of ourselves, we as Christians are a mass of weakness. But we hear afresh the promise of Christ to His church:

You shall receive power when the Holy Spirit has come upon you; and you shall be witnesses to Me in Jerusalem, and in all Judea and Samaria, and to the end of the earth. (Acts 1:8)

Great Resources for Christian Living— from R. C. Sproul

CHOSEN BY GOD 0-8423-1335-4
Gain insight into the doctrine of predestination through this clear, biblical presentation.

ESSENTIAL TRUTHS OF THE CHRISTIAN FAITH
0-8423-5936-2
Categorized for easy reference, more than 100 doctrines offer a basic understanding of Christianity.

FOLLOWING CHRIST 0-8423-5937-0
This combination of four power-packed books will challenge you to become a mature follower of Jesus Christ.

THE GLORY OF CHRIST 0-8423-1617-5
This intriguing focus on the life, person, and deity of Christ is third in Sproul's trilogy on the Trinity.

THE HOLINESS OF GOD 0-8423-1365-6
A best-selling treatment of what is perhaps God's least understood dimension is developed in this first volume in Sproul's trilogy on the Trinity.

IF THERE'S A GOD, WHY ARE THERE ATHEISTS?
0-8423-1565-9
Here is excellent guidance for Christians who have doubts or who want to respond intelligently to skeptics.

THE INTIMATE MARRIAGE 0-8423-1610-8
Develop marriage skills that will lead you past potential problems into joyous communion with your spouse.

THE MYSTERY OF THE HOLY SPIRIT 0-8423-4378-4
Second in Sproul's trilogy on the Trinity, this book covers the role and nature of the Holy Spirit.

PLEASING GOD 0-8423-5024-1
The author shows how God delights in those who seek after righteousness.

THE SOUL'S QUEST FOR GOD 0-8423-6088-3
Find deeper intimacy with God through obedience to him and the power of the Holy Spirit.

SURPRISED BY SUFFERING 0-8423-6624-5
With concern for biblical truth, Sproul addresses the afterlife and the role of suffering in human experience.